A Special Calling...

*My path to teaching Special Education
and the memoirs of those years*

A Special Calling...

My path to teaching Special Education and the memoirs of those years

Barbra Badger

A Special Calling . . .
Barbra Badger, Badger Books
Copyright 2018

All rights reserved.

No part of this book may be reproduced or transmitted in any form or by any means electronic or mechanical, including photocopying, recording, or any information storage and retrieval system without permission in writing from the author.

ISBN 13: 978-0998243818
ISBN 10: 0998243817

Barbra Badger worked for twelve years as a teacher of profoundly developmentally disabled youth in public school settings. Now that she is well into retirement, her students are still very much a part of her thoughts and concerns. This book is an effort to share some insights, memories, and even worries about the young people who were entrusted to her.

This book will be of tremendous help to parents and educators because it was written from the heart of someone who has truly been there. The author's words ring true with her profound compassion, hard-won wisdom, searing frustrations and occasional moments of joy.

The book will also serve as an eye-opening admonition to those who mean well but are quick to say, "But why don't they just ..." without really understanding the students, their issues, their families, and their lives.

The book was not easy to write nor is it easy to read.
For writer and reader alike, it is well worth the effort.

Barbara Marino, M.A. School Administration, and

Susan Millett, PhD, Curriculum Development and Bi-Lingual Education

DEDICATION

A project like this should be dedicated to the people it concerns. Due to the confidentiality teachers must observe about their students, I cannot name all those who showed me how to be their teacher. The education required and the practical application of said studies often take priority. Then something out of the ordinary happens that brings the focus squarely on the student and a teacher's immediate response to them.

Special Education students can show us what they need most by how they respond to their environment and to us. Most of the time they need us to "see" them—truly see their inmost selves—and accept them with whatever foibles they possess by seeing past those shortcomings. The rest of the time, teachers will need to "listen" to their sounds, their silences, and watch closely what they do and our reactions to them.

For all my students, their parents, my assistants, ALL of them—my principals, the nurses, physical therapists, occupational therapists, psychologists, caregivers and bus drivers—God bless and keep you and those you love ... and thank you from the bottom of my heart.

ACKNOWLEDGMENTS

My husband suggested, nudged, encouraged, and supported this project. He stood by me during my most difficult personality modifications caused by the stress and angst the job put me through. My employer sent me several informational "flyers" regarding places I could get help, but the time and distance to achieve it was not doable.

But I must take this time to thank them for their efforts. In addition, my editor, Jenny Margotta, and one of my former assistants helped me keep things in order while I stumbled through a confusing past.

TABLE OF CONTENTS

Preface i
One Success Story—1998 1
Getting Started—Mid-Eighties 5
Another Odd Coincidence 11
How Severe Is Severe? 14
One Student—Many Issues 16
Paul Erases a Prejudice 19
Miracles Abound 22
Amber Signing A Song (NOT Singing) 24
Sam and His Mother 29
Joey 31
Learning About Runners '87-'89 32
Public Law 94-142: 35
The Education for All Handicapped Children
      Act of 1975 35
Individuals with Disabilities Education Improvement
      Act of of 2004 35
   Purposes 49
   Overrepresentation of Minority Children: 37
Free and Appropriate Public Education 38
Revelations from Randy 39
Spoiler Alert! Difficult Story 41
   Martha: 41
Shhhhh! Don't Tell the Principal! 44
Some Random Thoughts and
      "Happy, Happy, Happy" Ending 45
LOCAL-ARC: Working with Developmentally Disabled 49
vocational Clients 51
   Wes: 51
   Carlos: 52
   Yvonne and Carol: 55

    Kenny and Freddie: 56
    Donny: 57
    Mike: 62
Positive Memory 64
Back to the Classroom: 1998-99 School Year 65
Split-Second Timing 66
Runners at the High School Level 72
Follow-Up on Wayne 77
A Silly Story 78
Transformation of Mark and Me 79
Zeke and the "Good Year" 84
Toby—A Tragedy 90
An Unforgettable Person 94
The Stories of the Two Jo-Jos 96
    Jolene 96
    Stanley Jo 98
Mainstreaming At the High School 100
Helmlichs 102
Predictability 104
Little Kids—A Temporary Transfer: 106
Sally 109
Permanent Transfer—2004 112
    Main Findings from This Study: 114
    "Learn the Signs. Act Early." Program: 115
    About Developmental Disabilities and this Study: 116
    Developmental Disabilities—CDC Activities: 116
I Expected Something Magical 118

"LEARN THE SIGNS. ACT EARLY."

Identifying developmental disabilities early allows children and their families to get the help they need. You can follow your child's development by watching how he or she plays, learns, speaks, and acts. Talk with your child's doctor at every visit about the milestones your child has reached and what to expect next.

Learn more at www.cdc.gov/actearly.

Perfect your Heimlich technique and teach it to any caregiver in charge of your child.

PREFACE

A question often asked of me—which I am never sure how to answer—is, "Did you choose Special Ed or did it choose you?" Perhaps, after you've read the information in this book, you may have an opinion. I'm still on the fence about it.

When I was four, a man with cerebral palsy lived across the street. He was my introduction to people who appeared different. I was too young to go to school and was living with my grandmother and great grandmother. That arrangement resulted in me spending much of my time outdoors.

I saw the man walking one afternoon. He was inside a large frame of metal tubes with wheels. Those early assistive walkers were quite cumbersome. He didn't look or move like anyone I knew or had ever seen, but I could tell he was a person. There we were, he and I. Out in the big wide world, enjoying the sunlight and air and fellow beings. I smiled and waved at him.

His reaction when I waved was a joyful response to being acknowledged. Reaffirming his sameness as a human being created an engram in me that could never be altered. "Differences are not to be feared." Even the strange contraption that was holding him up couldn't keep his humanity from being obvious to me.

Afternoons during my kindergarten year I would set my stuffed animals in a semi-circle around my record player and "teach" them. The desire to be a teacher came and went in my elementary years.

Several people with various forms of being 'different' drifted through my life experiences.

A Special Calling ...

In high school I didn't aim for college because my teachers implied it was too difficult to get in for those of us—females—not skilled in math. I was on the cusp of the generation that broke all norms and overcame the restrictions that kept women from aiming for greater heights, before most of us knew it was possible. We were stuck in roles which many of us were never meant to occupy.

I did take a writing class at the local college—I was very pregnant at the time—and I enjoyed the class. But after the baby was born, our circumstances changed a lot, and college was out of the question.

The first class I took with the mindset of a serious college student was Medical Terminology. I loved that class, which proved to be very valuable for the rest of my life. I also took a class on the history and development of the Bible—which was more directing for future need.

College was a challenge that required me to keep chipping away at my fears and self-doubts. My personal life was also challenging at that time, and although I didn't know it, I was battling clinical depression.

Nevertheless, biology, anatomy, and physiology courses inspired me. An unexplainable force stirred within, and I hungered for all the knowledge I could grasp in those subjects. With the terminology and hospital experiences which came later, as a foundation, I aimed my sights at a medical career. That didn't happen, but whoever is in charge of directing me on my path knew what I would need, what I would love, and what I would keep for future use.

Some influences came from teachers whom I wanted to emulate. But the guidance continued throughout my life. Whenever I veered from the path chosen for me, my life and my psyche suffered. (Case in point: I was trained as a nurse's aide by the county and hired as soon as I completed the training, but I left to go live with my boyfriend in another town.)

I could say that even the job I had doing electronic assembly work fit into the guidance theme, but that is a stretch. It did provide me with skills to survive when no other means were available. And I met my current husband doing that work. Yet it wasn't until I was in the midst of my working life that I began to evaluate and appreciate that guidance. Once I realized how intricate the plan had been, it took my breath away—and it still does. I was amazed to discover that "someone" had been planting the seeds of acceptance in one so young and patiently steering me this way and that.

My frustration at not getting a good job when I received my bachelor's degree was matched by my disappointment. Human Services was dead in the Reagan Years, and I only had a few units to complete my degree in that field at the time. All doors seemed to be closed to me. I wanted a good-paying job. There were none to be had, forcing me to put in applications for not-so-good paying jobs.

That included working as an instructional assistant in schools, and sigh—as a nurses' aide. I am not in any way disrespecting the admirable spirit of nurses' aides everywhere or looking down on that incredibly difficult job. But our society implies there is greater reward for higher education. My heart was set upon some form of social work. My childish ego was sorely disappointed. Apparently, my soul needed the exercise in humility ... it still does.

After six months as a nurses' aide at a convalescent home and interactions with a nurse's knowledge of various medications and management of patients with dementia, Parkinson's, strokes, and other neurological maladies, the groundwork was laid for future encounters with people with severe cognitive impairments. When ethical issues at the facility got too far out of balance, I left. I went on the job hunt again.

It was a long and twisting path to finding my work in Special Ed, but when I got there it seemed like that was where I was meant to be...at least at first.

The following are stories of that tumultuous path, as I recall them from decades past. Finding a starting place was difficult because so many of these stories are tragic. Giving the reader, a positive start seemed to be the best thing. Out of the successes, I chose one that can be attributable, for the most part, to my efforts.

Other positive stories are the result of an assistant, or a combination of my helpers, the students' meds, and natural maturing.

The first story is actually in the middle of my teaching years. After that it goes back to my childhood and moves forward again from there.

Nothing would have pleased me more than to include photos of my students, but confidentiality negates doing that. Seeing those bright or mischievous faces would make for a better understanding of the level of need these students faced.

ONE SUCCESS STORY—1998

The first time I met Johnny he ran up to me, pursed his lips and blurted out "Bitch!" then ran away, chuckling. I would learn that he greeted all visitors that way. He was tiny for 14, slender and short. His smile was sweet, his gait slightly awkward.

Although for the most part Johnny wasn't aggressive, over the next few days with him, he revealed other unsavory habits. He thought it was very funny to expel gas and would make obvious movements when it was about to happen. The running up into someone's face and pursing of lips, and the motion before expelling gas are known as "precedent" behaviors. If you are sensitive and observant you can work with a precedent behavior and cut off the objectionable behavior at the pass. My helper and I started working on Johnny's right away.

Our room had furniture in place of desks. The room was entirely open like a great room, with two couches a love seat and a large ottoman in the carpeted living area. Included in that arrangement was a kitchen/dining area with a refrigerator and stove.

Also, in the kitchen area there were two, 7-foot tables and a computer desk we eventually used for sorting tasks and similar activities. There were other miscellaneous items in our room because no one seriously thought of it as being a classroom. To be fair, few of my students would have been able to take advantage of a stereotypical classroom setting.

Johnny's favorite place was on one of the couches. If anyone sat too close he would swipe the air with a clawed hand in front of the person's face, but I don't think he ever hit a student. Johnny liked to inspect things his curiosity was a strong suit. He could hold books without tearing them and he liked to paint.

When I started working in this classroom, I had two female assistants, who had been in this classroom all school year and knew all the students. For the most part it worked out fairly well.

One morning during summer school, my youngest, most inexperienced assistant began tormenting Johnny. I watched until it was clear that Johnny was no longer feeling just "teased" and it had become bullying. When Johnny started throwing chairs and everything else he could get his hands on, I sent the assistant out of the room

It was actually my first effort at taking control of the class. Since I was new to this room I wanted to observe as long as I could before taking the reins full on. The assistant left the room and Johnny was squealing and wildly clawing the air. I stepped into the windmill of his arms and hugged him. He pounded me on my back with his fists a few times then began to cry.

While standing there holding him, I noticed that one of those miscellaneous items in the room was a real desk for students. I had Johnny help me move it to an open space. I made him a nameplate and put papers, crayons, and some other favorite things in the desk. He was delighted, became easier to work with, and more cooperative in general. Doing that taught me that each student of this caliber needs their own 'spot'. Finding their own space helped keep things safe and peaceful.

We worked on his habit of running into people's faces and saying the "B" word, and every time he motioned to expel gas we sent him to the bathroom. I'm not sure how long it took, but by the time the next school year came, Johnny was dusting shelves in the library, sitting in the library with a book when he was finished. The regular education students went on about their own tasks and he blended right in.

Before Johnny left my classroom, all bad habits were

gone, and he had taught me another valuable lesson as well.

One of my bad habits was to react negatively in a knee-jerk fashion whenever I perceived something messy was about to happen. Working with Johnny helped me minimize that.

Johnny had succeeded in overcoming his rude habits, and the class was working on an art project for Halloween. Since this was a high school, Halloween was a big thing—and for us to take part would be welcomed.

I was sitting at the big tables, working with another student. Johnny was puttering around near the windows. My attention was all on the student beside me, since I was working hand over hand to help him paint—not tear the paper, eat the brush, or spill anything.

The back wall of our room was two-thirds windows. with a blank wall between. Those windows had advantages and disadvantages, of course, but they were a good thing for the most part.

When I looked up, Johnny had filled his brush with paint and was painting the windows. I almost jumped up and made him stop. But before I did that, I marveled at the fact that he had:

1. Taken initiative
2. Was not painting wildly, but purposefully
3. Had a serious expression, not mischievous

My helpers and I let him paint. When he had gone home, I smoothed out a few edges, added some minor details, and it became a recognizable jack o' lantern. I think I also added Johnny's name and showed him the results the next day.

One day he did something very unexpected. I was talking to the psych assigned to our students and Johnny came up with a juice box. He said something I 'assumed' was, 'what is this'? His level of understanding was limited to 'what' questions or so I thought. I answered, "a juice box." He walked away staring at it.

A few minutes later he came back and said it again

and I answered again. We both maintained a quiet, calm demeanor.

When he returned the third time, I 'heard' his request differently and knew that he had understood my previous replies and it was I who was not getting it. This time I heard him say, "Who is this?" a question a step above his level. I got totally energized and said, "It's Michael Jordan!" This time he smiled broadly as he walked away. I was thrilled.

After learning those lessons from Johnny, I found other occasions to let it be so the student could have a fully independent experience. One case was to let a blind student explore a collection of picnic tables being rearranged for the next school year. He had a cane and used it pretty well. We let him wander through the maze of a dozen or so tables, tapping and feeling his way with no assistance or interference from us.

It gave me a chance to observe his skill level and also determine his level of independence in a new environment. He explored for a long time, and I don't think he ever called for us. That was not a good thing, because he was extremely vulnerable. He was in a strange place and as far as he knew completely alone. The student's name was Toby, and he lived in a group home. He was blind from birth, walked very slowly, and had few words—one of which was "walk." We would take him out walking several times a day. There will be more about Toby later on.

For now, I will go back to the beginning and an odd coincidental phone call.

Note: You will read about me 'observing ' my students more than you will read about me interacting with them. The interactions were basically so redundant it would put you to sleep. Hand over hand practices of sorting, assembling, eating, wiping, are just a few of what I did all day. I also did changing diapers, cooking, cleaning up after, preparing activities, planning, repairing, problem-solving of computer glitches and equipment of various kinds and adapting things for my students to use. Add into this maintaining the usual attendance, toileting, seizure charting and directing staff—these were my most routine activities I chose not to include. One thing which I did NOT do, was sit in my 'office' on a regular basis.

GETTING STARTED—MID-EIGHTIES

This chapter starts before I was qualified as a substitute or credentialed for any sort of teaching job. When I left the convalescent home, I still wanted to work in Human Services. State, county and city levels had openings so I applied. How I got the job was one in a series of coincidences that had me believing I had been "chosen" for the work.

The first strange coincidence was a phone call from a school district.

Ring. Ring.
Me: "Hello?"
Phone voice: "Barbara?"
Me: "Yes."
Phone voice: "They need you in Mrs. Sizemore's class at Sierra Hills School tomorrow morning at seven-thirty."
Me: "Where is that exactly?"

The phone voice gave directions. I went to work the next day.

I had been working in the classroom as an instructional assistant for two weeks when it became clear the main office and payroll had no paperwork for me and didn't know who I was! I went down to personnel, took the required tests, filled out all the other important papers, and worked in that class the rest of the year.

During the time I had been unemployed with a fresh bachelor's degree for several months, I had probably applied there, along with dozens of other places. However, all record of that had been lost. I will never know how that phone call reached me.

The class was described at the time as Learning

Handicapped. It was a middle school and near the end of the year. Mrs. Sizemore was retiring that year and the district asked me to come back in the fall to introduce the kids to the new teacher and to be a bridge. Before she left, Mrs. Sizemore suggested that I take the special test the state was offering and become a substitute teacher. I mulled that over for a while and, in the meantime, kept the job in her classroom.

Mrs. Goldman came in the fall, and her style was the exact opposite of Mrs. Sizemore's. My own style had already been molded by Mrs. S., and it didn't harmonize well with Mrs. G. When we discovered that, I took the test to be a substitute and left her class. However, before I left, a series of very memorable events took place.

On my way home one day, I chose a route that I hadn't taken before. It was away from the well-trafficked streets and had some nice scenery. The fact that it was away from busier paths attracted some of the boys in our class to use it as a downhill run for their skateboards. There had been an accident of some sort, and one of the boys was knocked off his board and slid down the asphalt on a steep portion of the road. He scraped a lot of skin off his hands, and we discovered later—after being in my car for a while—that he had had an accident in his underwear.

I took the boys to a hospital to get seen. One of the boys called his mother, who told the other mothers about it, and one of them picked up the boys. I believed that I had been guided to them, but I'm not sure they saw it that way.

Mrs. Goldman was the model of the teacher I had always wanted to be. Wise enough to know that patience would get more learning accomplished than efforts to control behaviors that are impossible to externally control. Sadly, I didn't achieve that level of wisdom or patience in that classroom.

There were many other best practices techniques she employed with the unruly students. When the students from that class moved up to the high school, she got feedback that

A Special Calling ...

they were the most well-mannered ever to come out of the Learning Disabled class at the San Phillipe School.

In October of our time together, a flyer came to the school stating participants were being sought for Arthur Mitchell's Harlem Dance Theater try-outs. Our kids were mostly from the Projects, and break-dancing was exploding through the population at the time. Mrs. Goldman suggested that some of our best break-dancers in the class go to the try-outs. The idea was they would go twice a week for two weeks and have dance lessons. At the end of that time, some students would receive a scholarship to attend Harlem Dance Theater for the summer—in New York.

Our guys made the cut to attend to the two-week tryouts, and a young lady from Regular Ed, who was a superb ballerina, came with us. I drove the group to Pasadena and back. It was close to Thanksgiving and dark at 5 o'clock as I drove them home.

At the end of the two weeks, our ballerina got a scholarship. The boys had their self-esteem boosted by a factor of 100. For a while I tried to be their coach and get them gigs with some other local entertainers I knew, but it became impractical.

When the local paper heard about their opportunity to have lessons from Arthur Mitchell, they wanted to do an article on them. We worked it out, and something almost miraculous happened.

The photographer brought tons of professional equipment to the school. The lights, umbrellas, strobes, and just watching them set up raised the level of anticipation and pure excitement.

We did the shoot when all the other students were in class, so there was lots of room for the camera equipment and for the boys to do their thing. They did some warm-up tricks, and then I put on the music for their routine.

Oh! My Gosh!

They were literally flying in mid-air and hanging there long enough to be able to tell that they were flying. The camera caught a shot of one of the boys with obvious G-forces pulling his cheeks back. The boys gave a perfect performance, with helicopters, caterpillars, flips, twists, and spins of every variety—and they never missed a beat.

Here is the best part. The paper came out just before winter break, and there they were on the front page, on top of the fold, flying in mid-air. It was the perfect Christmas present for the guys and their families.

After break, one of the boys had girls chasing him all the way back into the "retard" room.

How do you follow an act like that? It's difficult, if not impossible. It was for me, anyway. Mrs. Goldman was getting a handle on the class—with her method of patience and a good reward system. I took the test for being a substitute and moved on.

A bachelor's degree and a passing score on the CBEST were the only requirements to be any kind of substitute teacher. Oh, and a willingness to accept ANY assignment gets you into the Special Ed classes. As an aside, I once subbed in boys' high school PE. I stood outside, where they lined up for attendance, and I never entered the gym or locker room.

My husband was hired by a company that paid for us to be moved to the new locale. It was fortunate, since I had shot myself in the foot badly at my previous job, and a new start would be helpful.

I must tell you that shortly after we moved to this completely different environment, I went on Pilgrimage in Israel. I went with a prayer for guidance as to what to do with the rest of my life. Well, be careful what you ask for, and stand back, because the answer may come on like a hurricane. After the Pilgrimage I was introduced to a field of work I didn't know existed.

The first day I subbed in a classroom for students described as severe and profoundly developmentally disabled was a device by some higher power to lure me into the specialty. The children were all small and quiet and non-ambulatory.

The room was fresh and bright with sunlight, smelled of laundry softener, and the crib mobiles played their gentle melodies.

Children were in cribs or well-padded carriers, while attendants moved from one to another, changing the bedding and diapers and maintaining cleanliness and order.

Of all the other substitute teaching jobs I would have, this was truly a piece of heaven.

One of the helpers instructed me to work with a child by exercising the legs and arms, just like I used to do with my own babies. The class was for pre-school and elementary-aged kids, so they were all easy to lift, turn, or carry.

Throughout that first day of feeding, playing, positioning, and interacting with these little angels—none of whom could talk or walk—peace and fulfillment were mine.

From that first-class experience, I was hooked. Several more times that year they requested me, and it was my joy to go.

Then came my long-term assignment. The class was described as Communicatively Disabled, and it was for pre-school children who were old enough to talk but were having difficulty expressing themselves, either because of pronunciation or shyness. Most were quiet and well-behaved for their age, but it only takes one with anger issues to trash a classroom. We had one. He was completely unsociable and would follow us to the staff restroom. He was aware of what he was doing and would open the door when we had sat down. For emergency purposes, no inner doors of the rest room could be locked. One afternoon, he pulled the blinds off the windows and tossed furniture generally destroyed the room. He was five.

I was in that room all summer and part of the fall. Two positive things stand out from that time, one of which I got to do a lot of art with them.

The day was divided into Large Motor Activities and Hand/Eye Activities, Speech, with time for imaginative play, outdoor play, story time, snack time. A special day I remember best a little girl came into our room, hopping like a frog. She had cerebral palsy and was bright but needed reminders to keep her tongue in. She was also learning to crawl, stand, and walk.

At recess she sat beside me on the sidewalk while we watched the other children taking turns on the slide. One after another, they climbed, slid, and got back in line to slide again. I looked down at her while she watched almost without blinking at the endless stream of children. When there was a break in the action, I picked her up, climbed the ladder, set her on my lap, and down the slide we went. After a few more times, I felt like I had tapped into something within me that could be nurtured and expanded into something really useful.

By sensing her wish to do the slide, and instinctively making it happen, I felt I had found "my calling." I decided to get my teaching credentials for education—regular education. My long-forgotten wish to be a teacher revived and I was inspired to reach that goal. I was almost 40—but felt strong and confident enough to see it through. (Could it have been an after effect of Pilgrimage?)

The desire was quickly aided when a local site became a satellite for major colleges. One of them offered a teaching credential in nine months. I went for it.

However, the lovely times of those first few days with the quiet babies were rarely repeated during the two years I spent getting my credentials or the 12 years I taught Special Ed for students described as severe and profound. But I kept telling myself during student teaching for my regular ed credential and subbing that, "When I get my own classroom, things will be different," meaning the struggles to teach a group of students instead of responding to their challenge of authority would not exist. I would be able to do all kinds of creative things and make learning real and fun at the same time.

ANOTHER ODD COINCIDENCE—WITH A TWIST—AND ANOTHER TIMELY PHONE CALL

Now back to coincidences that got me into the first class I ever taught in which the students were labeled Severe and Profoundly Developmentally Disabled.

As soon as I earned my regular education credentials, my husband and I consulted on how far afield I should look for work. He said, "Everywhere." We were living in a fifth-wheel at the time and could—if we should decide to—pick up and roll on down the road.

There was nothing available that I succeeded in landing in our locale. One Sunday we drove almost a hundred miles from our house. I bought a Sunday paper there. (This was 1987. Newspapers were still a going concern and had lots of classified ads for employment. Ed-Join did not yet exist). As soon as I saw the ad for Special Ed teachers about 200 miles from our town, I knew it was my job. I said to my husband, "If you don't want me to work in (that town), I won't apply, but I know this is my job." My confidence was in spite of the fact that I knew I wasn't qualified for it. Many pieces of my life's puzzle fell into place right then, and a certainty filled me crowding out any doubts.

The town was near my husband's family, and he thought it would be fine for me to apply there. If I was hired, we would work out the particulars. As soon as I made an appointment for an interview I received a phone call from a friend who needed someone to care for her mother, who had ALS. This friend lived in the same area where I had just applied for My Job. My friend was moving to England, and when she was settled there, she would move her mother over; meanwhile, she just needed someone to be with her mother at nights and on weekends.

As it turned out, I was a day late for the interview, had to wade through 18 inches of water, and therefore, I was soaked from my knees down when I walked in. But destiny had its way and well, I got the teaching job and would have room and board at my friend's house.

Oh—here's a little something I didn't know about until after I had signed the papers accepting the job. In order to keep it, I had to go back to school for the credentials I was required to have in order to teach that level of students.

I was 42 and had just earned my regular education credentials. I really, really, really, didn't want to go back to college. But my husband and I talked it over, and I decided to go for it. Earning the additional credentials would keep me away from home at least two years. The Master's in Teaching Special Ed with a specialty in Severe and Profound was only a few credits more, so I got the master's.

Esther, the sweet lady with ALS, was a Godsend for what I was doing. Many things that would plague my students also made her uncomfortable. The major difference however, was that my students were all non-verbal, while Esther could tell me if she was too warm, too cold, if the covers were rubbing her toes, or any number of things that a person does not think of if it's not happening to them. For example, laying on a wrinkle for hours becomes very uncomfortable. The awareness of that made me remember to smooth out clothing before putting a child in a wheelchair or some other position for long periods.

There were several times when a student would act strangely or give some indication that something was wrong, just nothing we could see. We would take off their shoes and socks and look for toenail troubles and work our way up, looking for bug bites or places where clothing might be pinching. The sources were numerous, and we found and

A Special Calling ...

solved the issues most of the time, thanks in large part to dear Esther.

Although it was a Special Ed position, I was still in elementary teacher mode and, while I was setting up my first classroom, I was making plans for activities that I eventually discovered none of my students could or would be capable of preforming. My principal wrinkled her brow when I told her I was sorting a jumble of items into shapes and colors. I had just spent nearly a year being drilled and trained for elementary teaching. This first classroom was an elementary level class, and although I knew they weren't going to be reading or doing science projects, I thought sorting and naming objects would be possible. As it turned out, I still had no clue what these students' goals would be. It was going to take a while for my brain to gear down.

Since the principal's expression was strong enough to read, and she said nothing about my accomplishment, I thought it was time to look at the Individual Education Plans (IEPs). I had had some introduction to them in the Learning Handicapped class, but since I was not the teacher, and all information is confidential, I really had no idea what was in them or how to write one. I learned that one real fast.

The goals in the IEPs were something like this: By 00/00/0000, Student will: take two bites of food with a spoon independently without spilling or, in some cases, throwing the spoon. OR: By 00/00/0000, Student will sit for 30 seconds in one spot, 3 times a day, with a 10-minute walk for reward.

So much for shapes and colors.

HOW SEVERE IS SEVERE?

You may be wondering, "What does 'severe' mean?" Or "Why are these children even in school?"

The most severely affected of my first students was a young girl who was homebound, too sick to be transported to school. Homebound or hospitalized students are assigned to teachers who see the student after regular school hours. I met her a few months before her death. One of her goals was to hold a marble for three seconds.

Several of my students' goals, like hers, were simply to "look at" or "gaze" or "follow with their gaze" an object in front of them. The point of training their gaze is just that: helping them focus deliberately on one thing. Once that is accomplished, you move to the next step. Depending on the ability of the child, the wishes of the parent—tricky, this one—and the logic involved, the next step could be a variety of things. For instance: reach for, grasp, or vocalize as requested.

A week after Carrie, my homebound student met this goal, she passed away. I visited my old classroom a few years later and found that her mother had become an instructional assistant there. She had another child who was born normal.

What makes the situation even more tragic is Carrie's mother kept telling the doctors that something was wrong because the child's head was getting too big. They were a Hispanic family, and the mother's pleas were ignored until the child had a seizure and went into a coma. By then too much damage had been done, and many organs had been affected. The child lived two more years with a trach, stomach tube, and 'round-the-clock nursing.

If you are not in the field, a parent of a child with these needs, or don't know a child with these needs, I know what you are probably thinking. What are these kids doing in school besides taking money that could be used for other classrooms? Why not put them in a hospital for people with similar disabilities?

Parents of these children—my students and the many thousands of others—worked tirelessly to put legislation through that gives their children the right to a free and appropriate public education, regardless of disability. There are other choices: one would be to keep them at home, which is a very costly venture and means that one parent must stay home, in addition to providing 24-hour nursing. Another choice—and here you must put yourself in the parents' shoes—is to put the child in an institution.

At the time I began teaching, that was still an option, although things were moving swiftly to move people out of warehousing conditions—where dozens or hundreds of the disabled were housed—to group homes where eight was the maximum in each house. A major problem was setting up group homes in the first place. That could not happen quickly, because they were private concerns taking on tasks previously handled by the State. To get the most reimbursement for services, a group home has to come into compliance with Federal regs and be inspected at regular intervals. Certification could be revoked if the home did not meet stringent requirements. But reimbursement from Medicare was most lucrative therefore, most owners went for that option.

ONE STUDENT—MANY ISSUES

The most difficult student I ever had to deal with in my very first class, was Tim. I have a question to pose to The Universe. Since you apparently chose me for this work, why would you challenge my weakest aspect? Why not let me use what I already had instead of stressing me beyond my capacity for patience? *

Tim was so severely mentally affected that he spent his mornings at another site for one-on-one attention before coming to my room, with another one-on-one assistant. He stimmed[1] by holding his hands near his mouth, cupping them toward his ears, and screaming. Some people in Special Ed aren't bothered by such noise; I was extremely bothered by it. Tim had other behaviors, like running out of the room, and pica, which were easier to shape into something useful.

Pica is an affliction that causes the person to eat everything. Not literally, in most cases, although I heard of a student who took bites out of tables. It causes the person to pick things up off the floor, ground, or sidewalk, and it goes straight into the mouth. Some will pick their diapers apart and eat those. Another student—I will tell more about him later—could not have a blanket on him in the hospital. He would eat

---

* An answer came: "Patience was not the point. The lesson was delegation--learning to use the help you were given.[1]

STIM: Any of various repetitive actions, such as flapping the hands, wiggling the knees, shining a light into one's eye, and spinning in a chair. Read more at #wiktionary# VwKQ2Sq0cLAbPpr7.99
http://www.yourdictionary.com/stim

it, and he was usually in the hospital because of some horrendous thing he ate that injured his digestive system.

The cause of Tim's overall disability was some mega infection his mother had had while she was pregnant. At the time, it was assumed he was constantly shedding the virus. When the nurse for our school became pregnant, she could no longer be near him or touch him because it was thought her baby might be as affected.

To this day Tim remains an enigma to me. The only skill we could find to build on was his pica tendencies, and we trained him to help clean up the campus. To meet our goal with Tim, an assistant would take him outside. Tim would pick up litter for a specified time, then get a designated time on the swings and return to class. It helped keep his tendency to run out of the room down to a minimum. There was nothing to be done about his screaming.

During my first year, we were encouraged to make home visits, and the following year—which was my last at that school—it became a requirement. When I visited Tim's "home," it was evening. Part of the requirement was to make observations and write down anything that stood out for further reflection. Doing this helped to make the IEP fit the student's reality.

This boy was in a large "care facility" intended for seniors who could no longer care for themselves, but they also had younger people who for one reason or another weren't sent to state institutions. The State had barely begun the process of transferring people out of the institution to smaller, more manageable facilities, and Tim and a few others were still housed there with the seniors.

The things that stand out in my memory of this visit I can't tie together very well. But here are those pieces.

The "feeding" time felt more chaotic to me than the disarray that took place in my classroom. Some patients were feeding themselves, and a woman was feeding my student in an overcrowded, too small room with peeling paint and little if any furnishings. Those feeding themselves were in their wheelchairs; my student wouldn't sit in any chair, so he was on the floor.

I don't recall the transition from there to "bath" time, but I do remember a girl of about 20 being taken to the bathing area by the same woman who had fed my student. While the girl was being bathed, Tim was pounding on the metal tub she was in. I recall the young patient being aware enough that she was embarrassed by my presence, and I backed out of sight. I can't imagine having to be bathed while someone was bashing on your tub.

Tim had to stay with the attendant because he could never be left alone—and there was not enough staff to cover that much personal attention and care for the other 99 patients.

The only other memory I have from that visit is the toilet. I had to use it before leaving. The walls were in such disrepair that I could see the outside while sitting on the commode.

I heard that Tim was sent to a group home out of that district the following year. I also heard he was doing well and making progress in controlling his behaviors.

PAUL ERASES A PREJUDICE

When I was in the fifth grade, there was a boy who had so many freckles you could barely see any skin other than them. I lived in Iowa then, and one winter day he followed me home and threw snowballs at me. Each one got harder until, finally, one had a rock inside. It hit me in the back of the neck and went under my clothes and down my back. From then on I've had a knee-jerk response to males with lots of freckles. It was an instant negative attitude, and I avoided them whenever possible.

The first of my students on my first day of school was Paul. He was in his wheelchair, his torso lying on his tray with his eyes closed and his face in a pool of drool. His face was also generously covered in freckles! That knee-jerk response of "Ugh!" hit me! The drool didn't bother me at all—it was the freckles.

Then he lifted his head in slow motion, like many people with cerebral palsy tend to do, and turned his head toward me. I said, "Paul," and his blue eyes opened in concert with the rising of his head. When he saw me, his mouth opened as wide as any mouth can, and he beamed a smile at me I can still see as clear as day. No more prejudice against boys with freckled faces!

Paul was capable of using switches to operate computers for games. These games were for increasing hand/eye coordination or for matching simple objects. When I first came to his room—yes, it was *his* room—he was very adept at using those switches. As time went on, his body grew but his strength did not, and it became harder for him to accomplish things that he had previously been able to do.

Paul had a game he liked to play and would do it a thousand times a day. He would tip his head back and stare at the ceiling until you looked up, and then he would laugh with a squeal of delight that was unmistakably pure joy. Every new person who came into the room or met his gaze at all would be subjected to his game.

Grinning, with a hint of mischief in his eyes, he would tip his head back and look up at the ceiling. Invariably, the person would also look up. Then Paul would giggle and squeal. He'd continue to do that until the person caught on that Paul was in control of this game. Being in control was very important to him, and the game never ceased to be funny to him.

He had lots of special equipment in addition to his chair with the Plexiglas tray, the shoulder, torso, and head braces. One piece of equipment was something that made it possible for him to stand and move about—if he would have used his toes to move it. We put him in it nearly every morning and played songs that he could "dance" to. I would dance with him by pulling the stander all around, or sometimes I would just hold him in my arms and dance with him that way. He giggled the whole time, and the dance motions got his circulation going so he could be more alert the rest of the day. I had a boom box that played tapes for our music. It operated with little slide switches. He would maneuver over to it and with his tiny but very reliable index finger, he would slide the volume up to max. Students who had difficulty with loud noises complained while Paul chuckled.

My favorite story about Paul is about the many times I put him on the changing table in the bathroom, and he would roll onto one side, use that trusty index finger, point, and make a soft oooo sound. The room had a few stalls without doors and a few "adapted" toilets with all kinds of special added paddings, belts, etc.

He kept this up, until one day I became thunderstruck: he was pointing at the adapted toilets and wanted to sit on them.

    The strangest feeling I have ever had came over me as I realized our minds had literally become one for a moment. We were both laughing and crying at the same time. "I bet your mom told you to tell me to do that, didn't she?" I asked. His expression and laughter confirmed it—another mind meld.

    From then on we put him on the toilet on a regular basis, and sometimes it was successful. Working with Paul, I learned about the myriad ways a person could be assisted with technology. Even at that time—a few decades ago—there was a plethora of switches. Some required merely a touch, others just a head movement or even less—a breath.

    Those that did require touch could be placed where the most functional part of the person could use it, and the degree of touch could be modified to the amount of pressure, the range of motion to move a head, hand, elbow, or foot, or breathe on a switch. And yes, there were folks who could only move one of their feet.

    About 10 years later, eye-gaze equipment had shrunk to a miniscule dot, and voice mechanisms and even more sophisticated types of switches were developed, freeing the most trapped inside to contact the world. I often wondered if Paul had been fortunate enough to have the opportunity to try them out. We met in 1987 and I left in 1989. Technology of all types has increased exponentially since then.

    To add more 'lightness' to these memories--We used to get a kite up and flying well, then attach it to Paul's wheelchair. He delighted in looking up and it helped him practice to keep his head up, strengthening his neck muscles.

MIRACLES ABOUND

Expos focusing on assistive devices for the disabled, was one of my favorite things to do in regards to working in Special Ed. I loved to learn about all the new technology. There were talking books and the newest wheelchairs for racing and other sports. There were switches and voice-operated objects even then, the late 1980s.

One thing at the first Expo is something I would love to have in my house. There is cabinetry that can be lowered and raised by a switch. I am a short person, and the builders of home cabinets are *not*; counters and shelves are always a few inches too high. When I was young I didn't think anything of it, but as I get older it becomes more of a nuisance to keep a small stepladder in the kitchen and drag it out every time I need to use the second shelf.

I could stay all day at those new technology Expos. Another moment that sticks in my memory is the first time I saw the light that reads your eye gaze. When the light source was turned on and calibrated for your eyes, you could type out words by holding your focus on a letter and the computer would type it on a screen.

I watched as the pitchman used it to show its accuracy. A lot of times, people who have cerebral palsy can't control their head movements, or they swivel or shake their head persistently, not being able to stop.

A man in a wheelchair, who had CP stopped by to watch the demonstration, and the salesman did something I could not believe. With that man sitting there in his chair—his head moving all about—the salesman asked *me* if I wanted to try it.

I declined. "I want to see him try it," I said.

What happened next astounded everyone watching. The man was positioned where the light beam could find him, and after a few false starts, his head sat perfectly still while his eyes moved about the virtual keyboard, and he wrote, "I cannot believe this is happening." Then he began to laugh and tossed his head all over the place with joy.

Hopefully, from then on the salesman used demonstrators who could most benefit from the device.

Objects my students could use, oddly enough, I would still have to adapt for them by making them bigger or smaller or more usable one way or another.

The last Expo I went to—for my most recent class—in 2004 had learning games and more items that were specifically designed for my students' levels. I bought a computer program for a student so she could make her own book. The manual for it required attending classes on how to use it, and the classes were two days' long. I bought the program and tried to learn the manual on my own time.

I don't remember whether or not the student got to make her own book. She was out a lot with surgeries to her hips. I vaguely recall that we did make her a book but wouldn't swear to it on a Bible.

AMBER SIGNING A SONG (NOT SINGING)

A disconnect occurred many times between parents' expectations, the child's skill level, and information from support professionals' test results.

Amber was eight when she and I first met. Born with severe Down's syndrome and years spent in conditions of neglect, she had lain for hours without being touched, being changed, or fed for the first four years of her life. The next two years her grandmother spent in court, attempting to gain custody of Amber. Courts were reluctant to remove children from their mothers at that time, regardless of deplorable conditions or other factors. However, Grandmother succeeded in getting custody after winning the State lottery. From then on Amber went to Disneyland, got new clothes frequently, and was thoroughly pampered.

Things change in Special Ed as progress is made in techniques of working with the population, advances in technology, philosophy, and laws pertaining to the physically and mentally challenged evolve.

At the time I was in Amber's classroom, there was a mandate to involve our kids with the Regular Ed kids. It is now called Inclusion, but steps were taken very slowly, and of all my students, Amber was the best candidate. Even though she stood on her toes too close people while she flapped her hands rapidly, she was personable and willing to interact with others. There was a little girl that came in during lunch and her recess to be Amber's buddy. I will call her Ruby because she was a gem—she was very quiet and didn't seem afraid of

Amber's exuberant behaviors.

Toward the end of the year, Amber played with the Regular Ed students on the equipment at recess. We were very close by to answer questions and help the children understand her limitations with speech and hearing. I don't remember any negative incidents. I do remember how happy she was to be out there with the other children. I think of it as a successful first effort at mainstreaming.

Since Amber's grandmother took her to Disneyland a lot, Amber responded to everything connected to it. One afternoon when the little girl came in the song "When You Wish Upon a Star" was playing, and I was signing it. Amber was picking up on it and signing it back. Now according to all her psych tests, she wasn't supposed to be able to do that.

I realize she could not understand the context or have any real comprehension of the words, but she could *copy*— and do it well. I believe she could have used a picture book with maybe 10 or 12 simple items, like Home, Grama, Drink, favorite foods or Toys to communicate.

The next day I signed a few simple words that weren't in the song and I asked her to sign them back to me. Even though she had hearing aids in both ears, she did a fine job.

When I told the psych about it, he discouraged me from continuing on that path, probably because he knew she had no comprehension of what she was signing. However, the connections could be made with repetitive practices between the picture and the object of choice. The man's discouragement didn't deter me, and since it was my last year in the class, I wanted to go out with a bang.

Every school has an awards program at least once a year, and ours was held at the end of the year. I told Amber's grandmother that Amber would be doing something special during the ceremony, so she dressed her in a beautiful pink, ruffled dress with matching everything, and as always, her hair and skin were shining and all her clothes were immaculate.

Ruby came to our awards ceremony, and when

everyone was quiet I played The Song. Amber followed her friends' signing and did so without once flapping or bouncing on her tiptoes. That may have been even more astonishing than the signing. Her grandmother was not the only one in need of a tissue, but her tears came from a place of wonder and gratitude. Whether Amber was ever taught any form of communication is unknown to me, but the moment she gave to everyone in that room that day is cherished in my heart.

My principal had told me she had hired me instead of one of the new, younger teachers so I could stand up to this grandmother and another Mom about my age, when they became demanding. It must have worked, because the demands they made on her dropped to nearly nothing. For the demands on me, however, this grandmother wanted me to change Amber's socks when her feet got sweaty, she wanted us to be sure that the child drank a quart of liquid every day, and I know there were other tasks she made that were equally impossible. Amber did not have or warrant a one-on-one aide for any other reason than to see to Grama's requests. We could not meet those requests, but we did try.

Why was it such a burden to do these things? To answer completely would take a separate volume since it requires detailed enumeration of every task that needed doing, in addition to mentioning the unknowns that occur and the thousands of questions and problems to be met on any given day.

Here is a short answer. My last year of teaching in that room, I had 11 students aged from 3 to 14. I had two runners, four or more non-ambulatory; none were self-toileting, several had recurring seizures, and only two could feed themselves. Those who couldn't walk had braces on their legs, their trunk, or their wrists that had to be removed for blocks of time and replaced. Those who were completely unable to move had to be repositioned several times a day. Then throw in changing diapers, toileting, attempting to work on IEP goals, feeding, cleaning the students and the room, chasing down the runners, keeping the right amount of clothing on each child,

A Special Calling ...

all while there may be very high-pitched screaming, head banging, or some other constant distracting noise. And number one—maintaining a safe environment.

Yes, my assistants were capable and helpful, but my inexperience in prioritizing and predicting problems was not yet developed.

Back to the reason I was hired. (To help manage the two older caregivers and keep them from involving the principal.) As it turned out, in my second year they both wanted to be Room Mother, and since I needed all the help I could get, I let them both be Room Mothers.

That had its pros and cons. The good part was I had a little extra help when I needed it. Good, homemade food and lots of healthy drinks were supplied by them. The price I had to pay came at the most harried part of our school year. As a result of their collaboration, Christmas in my classroom that year was more nerve wracking than usual. The less fortunate—wherever they are found around holiday time—are a magnet for those who want to help. Whether the recipients are economically disadvantaged, aged, or like my students, people want to give them a happy holiday.

I do not want to disparage anyone who is moved at any time to help out in whatever way they wish. But for me, at that time it would have been more helpful if they had found an angel tree or dropped off some gifts at the school.

The school where I was working was in a lower-middle-class neighborhood, and some of my students were bussed in from areas of poverty. The region was settled hundreds of years ago. If left to itself, it would be a desert. Amber's grandmother and her co-Room Mom decided to give the kids a white Christmas, with Santa Claus landing in a snow-covered playground—by helicopter. The snow-making machine was cranking it out as I drove up that day, and it made a lot of noise, but it didn't come close to what the helicopter could do. From the perspective of the kids who could enjoy it, that white Christmas was a wonderful thing. For the more autistic and the teachers—not so much. The audience was evenly split.

Children who have problems processing information or are overwhelmed by any sound that grates on their nerves don't do well with buses, microwaves, or fire alarms. Helicopters!!?? I learned that I could take my students out of any situation, but there was some social pressure involved for me as a "new" teacher to go with the flow and meet the expectations of the established staff, as well as the parents who devised the plan. For the rest of the year, my students came first.

Our over-crowded schedule meshed all of our students and most of the Regular Ed students clamoring around a helicopter and playing in the snow, while the teachers and aides of the special ed kids tried to keep our over-stimulated kids from escaping, attacking, or coming completely undone in the melee. Some of my students were cognizant enough to want to participate. This is done by hand-over-hand (HOH) manipulation so the student gets the general feel and sensations involved. Throughout my teaching, hand over hand was the "norm," and it is very time consuming, which made it difficult to tend to all the students' needs and provide HOH experiences every day.

Under these circumstances and with only a few assistants, not all students got a chance to fully experience the snow on their fingers making a snow angel, or getting up close to Santa Claus.

Paul got to be a snow angel, but it took two assistants to get him out of the chair, move his limbs for him and, while he was still covered in snow, put him back in the chair.

I took the children who were upset by it all back to the room and didn't bow to social pressure again. In circumstances when I knew my students couldn't handle it, we didn't go or I sent one or two out with an assistant.

SAM AND HIS MOTHER

Teachers are mandatory reporters of suspected child abuse. We should also report when children's living circumstances appear to put them in danger.

Sam, who was blind, non-ambulatory, and non-verbal, came to my class. He was about 10 and very close to normal size. His mother was on the low end of the mental-ability scale and, due to her inability to provide a safe environment, already had a daughter in foster care. The mother and Sam were living with her boyfriend, and their shelter was near one of my other students' home.

Sam was a good boy who never rebelled or had any aggressive tendencies. Every day when he came to school, we would bathe him because he had dirt and grit all over himself and his clothes. He first came to my class in November, and it was very cold.

I made arrangements to visit the place where they were living, and by all rights I should have had social services come and get him and take him right then. The "home" was in a small camper shell that had no windows. A double-wide trailer sat next to it but was unusable, not seated, or connected to water or power. Outside of the mobile home, there were tons of clothes in dozens of black trash bags—which had never been opened. For electricity, a cord ran from a house next to their camper. When the wind blew—and it blew a lot there—dirt from the vacant lots nearby came in and layered all over the bed where Sam slept.

The extension cord that ran from the house to the camper shell had a few other cords attached, and it lay on the sink. Fortunately, they didn't have running water. Sam's mother said they used the water from the house where the cord originated.

I told the mother she should make arrangements to have better housing as soon as possible. She promised they would be out by the end of the month.

The next day when I told the staff about the conditions, they suggested I call CPS right away. Instead, I gave the family a sleeping bag that was to be only for Sam and we continued to bathe him daily to get the grit off him.

The end of the month came and went. Then one day he came in with a bruise on his bum. It wasn't very big and was probably caused by someone accidentally sat him in the chair while the seatbelt was on the cushion.

It was the last straw and I called CPS. The police came and took pictures; in the Polaroid print, you could barely see the mark—if at all—and it had the distressing effect of looking like porn. A policeman; a caseworker from CPS; Sam's caseworker from Regional Center, and my principal came to my room. The caseworker from CPS took Sam away before the end of the school day.

None of the official people bothered to tell the mother what had happened and I was unaware of that. Everyone involved assumed someone else was going to do it. The next thing I knew I was being threatened by the boyfriend. "I'm gonna kill you," he told me. It was too traumatizing for me to remember the circumstances of the phone call, but my principal called all the teachers at our school together for a meeting and told them I had been threatened and to watch out for the man.

There was a timeline involved. The mother had promised me they would be out of the camper in two weeks' time. Of course, they were not and that was when I started looking for another reason. I never had to do that again.

JOEY

When Sam moved, it left an opening in my classroom. I was sent an additional runner, Joey, who was smarter, faster than my other runner, and without a one-on-one aide. He was nonverbal, but he understood nearly every word that was said to him. When he did run, he would trample those lying on the mats. He was just clueless not intentionally mean. He didn't have screaming issues—at least I can't remember any—but he spent a lot of time going out the door. For a little while, I had one boy going out the front and one going out the back, while we all had our hands full, changing or doing some other hands-on activity with other students.

At that time we were allowed to do a basket hold, which I used at those moments when I knew Joey was probably going to make a break for it. In a basket hold, you encircle the child with your arms, their back to your front. You take their right arm and cross it over their body to their left side and vice versa with the other. You are helping them hug themselves, while you hold their arms close to their body. It is most effective in a sitting position while legs are crossed. There are other several physical deterrents that are no longer allowed, I'm sure. But the basket hold saved my least capable students from being stepped on.

What would I do differently now? If and when at all possible, I would appoint and rotate my assistants to be a one-on-one aide for Joey, so long as everyone was consistent with the IEP or behavior plan. However, there weren't enough classrooms or teachers at that time to place all the students as properly as the law required.

LEARNING ABOUT RUNNERS '87-'89

Kids—most kids—have a special radar. Every parent knows even the youngest child has ways of demanding attention, usually when the parent is most unwilling or physically unable to give it. The older children get the better they are at it, since they have full use of their minds and bodies.

Runners—students who run out of the classroom or away from adult supervision at any and every chance—put themselves, the adults supervising them, and the students who will be left unsupervised if the adults chase them in jeopardy. Some runners have that special radar and hone it to perfection. They run during some other crisis or when the staff is thoroughly engaged with other students. However, not all of them are that aware.

Some are fast and determined and run several times a day. Others are mere opportunists, and slip out on an occasional whim.

A difficult arrangement is for a classroom to have two or more runners and two or more escape routes to choose from. When this happened to me, all my alarm bells went off in my head. Those bells are connected to the awareness that it was I who was ultimately responsible for the safety and welfare of all the students. That meant the ones who just left my purview, as well as the ones unable to do so. I felt an overwhelming need to split myself into several pieces so I could be everywhere at once and solve every problem—all day long.

I'm not sure when it happened, but somewhere along the way a Three Dog Night song came into my head. The song was a repetition of the phrase, "Celebrate, celebrate,

Dance to the music." I changed it to "Delegate" and repeated it to obsession. It worked for a while, but I reverted back to trying to do it all myself, so it didn't stick.

Coping skills develop over time and may not be in place when stress being caused from several different directions—meaning several students causing a danger at the same time or needing to be toileted, while another is having a seizure. Those skills usually come after the stress has been alleviated to a degree. Determining where is the greatest danger or the most critical emergency takes time to learn. However, some of what I came up with did not uphold the standards I expected of myself. I yelled a lot.

My introduction to danger for the runners was a disaster. Kenny came to us with the vocabulary of a sailor. He was the only student in my room who could speak, and he spent most of his words calling us names. He would run out of the room and threaten to jump off the roof of the building. He was only six and small for his age, and he could never pull that off, but he found something he *could* pull off and he did it.

Our portion of the school was at the lower end of a Regular Ed school campus, which had all the trimmings of swings, jungle gym, and sand areas. Our students would never use most of those things. We usually took our kids out to the sandbox when the other kids were in class, but none of the other equipment was appropriate for our kids.

I happened to be in an IEP meeting, and my new assistant—who was not only new to me, but to the field in general—followed Kenny, who had just run outside, to keep him supervised. Kenny was ahead of her, swearing at the top of his lungs as usual. As he ran toward the jungle gym, he was saying between swear words, "I'm gonna jump off the top." He did. The equipment was tall enough, and he was malnourished enough, that when he jumped, he broke his arm.

Coincidentally, I saw him again in his 20s, and he had lost all speech and most mobility. I was not privy to the details of how he became so much more severely disabled. It was a shock to see him that way. I shared with his teacher that he had been in my first classroom and how verbal and active he had been. She was baffled.

When he broke his arm, it was clear that a new teacher and an untrained assistant were not a wise choice—my principal gave me an experienced assistant and sent Kenny to another site. He was one of several students of mine over the years who had mental illness symptoms in addition to developmental delays—the term is dual–diagnosed—but he was not the last or most clinically affected.

* A reasor for some chronic runners may be too many people in a room. A successful method of dealing with that is to let them stay a distance away with full supervision—outside the room until they feel comfortable to come back into the room.

PUBLIC LAW 94-142: THE EDUCATION FOR ALL HANDICAPPED CHILDREN ACT OF 1975

On November 19, 1975, Congress enacted Public Law 94-142, also known as The Education for All Handicapped Children Act of 1975. Congress intended that all children with disabilities would <u>"have a right to education, and to establish a process by which state and local educational agencies may be held accountable for providing educational services for all handicapped children</u>."
    Initially, the law focused on ensuring that children with disabilities had access to an education and to due process of law. Congress included an elaborate system of legal checks and balances called procedural safeguards designed to protect the rights of children and their parents.

INDIVIDUALS WITH DISABILITIES EDUCATION IMPROVEMENT ACT OF 2004

Congress has amended and renamed the special education law several times since 1975. On December 3, 2004, the Individuals with Disabilities Education Act was amended again. The reauthorized statute is the Individuals with Disabilities Education Improvement Act of 2004 and is known as IDEA 2004. *

In reauthorizing the IDEA, Congress increased the focus on accountability and improved outcomes by emphasizing reading, early intervention, and research-based instruction by requiring that special education teachers be highly qualified.

Purposes:

The Individuals with Disabilities Education Act of 2004 has two primary purposes. The first purpose is to provide an education that meets a child's unique needs and prepares the child for further education, employment, and independent living. The second purpose is to protect the rights of both children with disabilities and their parents.

.*The statute is in Volume 20 of the United States Code (U.S.C.), beginning at Section 1400. The Special Education regulations are published in Volume 34 of the Code of Federal Regulations (CFR) beginning at Section 300.

Overrepresentation of Minority Children:

In 1975, Congress found that poor African-American children were over-represented in Special Education. These problems have persisted. In the Findings of IDEA 2004, Congress described ongoing problems with the over-identification of minority children, including mislabeling and high dropout rates:

(A) Greater efforts are needed to prevent the intensification of problems connected with mislabeling and high dropout rates among minority children with disabilities.

(B) More minority children continue to be served in special education than would be expected from the percentage of minority students in the general school population.

(C) African-American children are identified as having mental retardation and emotional disturbance at rates greater than their White counterparts.

(D) In the 1998-1999 school year, African-American children represented just 14.8 percent of the population aged 6 through 21 but comprised 20.2 percent of all children with disabilities.

(E) Studies have found that schools with predominately White students and teachers have placed disproportionately high numbers of their minority students into special education.

FREE AND APPROPRIATE PUBLIC EDUCATION AND HOW THAT TURNED OUT IN MY CLASSROOM

One part of the law relating to my students is the word appropriate. The basic statement is that these students shall receive a free and appropriate education.

That phrase was to mean that the child will be in a classroom with students of the same or near the child's own chronological age. Students who were eligible for severe and profound classes were grouped in the following ages: pre-school 3-5; elementary 6-11; middle school 12-15; high school 16-22. (In all cases, give or take a year.) Therefore, assuming the student doesn't move away during those blocks of time, a teacher can have a student for six years when they reach high school. The 22-age limit is contingent upon the student's birthdate. If it falls before a certain date—they age out at 21. If not, they stay until 22.

Conditions regarding meeting the requirement for placement of students in age-appropriate classrooms were extremely difficult at the time I was hired. in 1987. Not having enough teachers to meet the demand was one thing, but they also did not have enough classrooms for age-appropriate settings. When a school's catchment area has only one child of preschool age or one child in middle school age within an area, and no separate classrooms for either of them, but you have one classroom in elementary age (mine) in the area, what else can you do?

During my second year of training, I had a 3-year-old, along with 8 age appropriate elementary students, and by the end of the year I had 11 kids, which included a 14 year old.

REVELATIONS FROM RANDY—
THE THREE-YEAR-OLD

Here's what Randy, the three-year-old, taught me about sensory over stimulation.

He could hold a pencil and copy a drawing perfectly–not by tracing but just freehand. (Children are not expected to be able to hold a pencil correctly until 6 or after.) The drawing may have been a simple house rectangle, with a chimney and some windows, but he was only three, and you couldn't tell his from mine.

His abilities fascinated me. He had no speech and did a lot of stimming by twiddling his fingers in front of his eyes. He couldn't walk—not sure why—but he loved puzzles, and the ones we had were too easy for him. Most of the time he rolled around on the floor. I would have handled him very differently if he were my student today. I would order equipment to enable him to stand upright with no pain. Then I'd find any toys in his age group that kept his attention—probably anything with lights and sounds and worked with him to gain speech. There are many other helpful items to keep a student like Randy challenged and growing.

There are also weighted blankets and other sensory feedback tools that would help him--now.

Given the conditions I had at the time, and my lack of training, I did the best I could. I found an eight-piece floor puzzle that was four feet in size when finished. The floor worked well for him because sitting was not easy for him. The puzzle was of Big Bird, and of course, it was the brightest yellow in the spectrum. I spread it out for him and had to go do something else. He squealed at it and stimmed a lot. I looked over once in a while and he had not made any progress. This puzzled me—yeah, that's intentional.

Eventually, I had time to sit with him, and I did the puzzle a few times, thinking he would copy me. He just squealed and flicked his fingers in front of his face a lot. Somehow, a few pieces got turned over to the bland back side. He stopped squealing, turned over all the pieces, and completed the puzzle. I'm not sure if it was me or him who turned them all over to the back side, but he put it together faster than I could count. No squealing, stimming, or tantrums—just zoom, done.

After that session, I turned them over to the bright yellow side as an experiment, and the first thing he did was turn them to the other, bland side, then put it together in a flash.

I couldn't find any more floor puzzles that were age appropriate or fit his skills. But his lesson—which I took to heart and expanded to help me better understand other students—was: Sensory stimulation that comes from the outside manifests in many forms. Too much perfume, or Downy; sweatpants of the slick variety, or the squeal of another student could set someone off. The over-the-top input can be eased by removing the stimulus, and most of the time the person will calm down.

*No commercial internet at that time, a broader search could not could be done.

SPOILER ALERT! DIFFICULT STORY

Now a story that is hard to tell. There are a lot of them. The field itself generates them. The really positive ones are rare, and I have been sparing you, the reader, from the worst ones so far.

There are several stories in this collection that are extremely heartbreaking. Perhaps my preparation for the work was the heartbreaks which had occurred in my own life. It is almost as painful to tell today as it was to experience at the time.

Martha:

The first week of my first year, teachers were to choose a bulletin board to cover. One whole wall of 40 feet or so was up for grabs. I took about 10 feet of it and dazzled my principal when she saw life-sized outlines of my students as soon as she walked into our school.

We laid the students on the floor and drew an outline around each of them, then added detail later. Martha stood out because of a little fountain of hair right in the middle of the top of her head. Her mother fixed it that way every day. But it was distinctive to her and added to her cuteness. Martha didn't walk or talk, neither did she scream nor have any aggressive behaviors. She was a sweet child and made sounds that she felt were talking. Her demeanor and size made her like a little doll.

Martha came to school in a stroller. She didn't really need a wheelchair. The stroller added to the doll image.

My students arrived on several buses, and some of those buses carried normal-sized kids who went to the SED—Severe Emotional Disorder—class at a different part of the campus. Martha rode with one of those boys, a sixth grader who was as big as an eighth grader.

One afternoon I was tucking Martha into her stroller and arranging her clothes so she wouldn't be sitting on lumps for her long ride home. I could see the big boy watching us, and I felt something wasn't right but had no idea what at the time. His teacher mentioned to the bus driver that the boy had had a bad day, but nothing more was said.

The bus driver had no aide, and he had several wheelchairs to unload. The lift for them could be very slow at times, which left the rest of the bus unobserved for several minutes.

While the driver was chatting with a mom and doing all the necessary things to unloose one of the wheelchairs from the lift, inside the bus, the big boy grabbed a wheelchair tie-down—they have huge metal hooks on the end—and began beating Martha on the head with it. The driver said that Martha was not making any loud noises or anything; the big boy just suddenly starting whipping her with the metal hook and strap.

There were occasions when I had worked in SED classes as an instructional assistant, and I had quickly decided it was not for me. I could find no compassion for them and accepted no excuses from them for their actions. Having left all forms of classrooms, I can now rationalize for them, but if I had to deal with them every day, I'm sure it would turn out badly for all involved.

The next day when Martha didn't come to school, my principal called me to the office to tell me what had happened. I was speechless, horrified, and yes, heartbroken.

Deep down inside I remember when I was five, six, or seven and feeling jealous rage at seeing someone my age getting an outpouring of tenderness from someone. I never acted on it, but even being able to relate to that feeling, I still could not find empathy for big boy.

The boy's teacher brought him over and had him apologize. I knew he didn't mean it, and he knew I didn't mean it when I let him off the hook.

When Martha returned, she was wearing a soft helmet until the stitches in her head were taken out. The big boy's teacher suggested Martha should wear it as long as they rode the bus together. Because no one could know what the trigger was, the district put an aide on the bus ... talk about too little too late!

Paul rode the same bus, and he was afraid of the big boy, so they always put Paul's chair right behind the driver.

SHHHHH!
DON'T TELL THE PRINCIPAL!

Every Friday we would have food fights in this classroom. Instigated by me. The boys in the wheelchairs got the biggest kick out of it, especially when chocolate pudding, catsup, and mustard got involved. All colors of Jell-O, mashed potatoes, pureed sweet potatoes, or peas made a rainbow of goo, splotching faces, chests, hair, towels, chairs.

We draped the boys with towels, filled spoons with food, and using hand over hand they flipped it at each other, to their endless delight. I got to blow off steam, and they got some moments of being "normal" 8-10-year-old boys. I didn't include the girls because they didn't want to be included, and if catsup, etc. got in their hair, it would be hard to explain, and we didn't have time to wash and dry them. When I saw Paul's lips turn blue from laughing, that's when we had to stop.

I didn't do this in the high school, because safety was job #1 and the boys were ambulatory and much bigger. They also didn't have the capacity to enjoy such activity, but I didn't think of it at the time. The messes would have been a lot harder to clean up. If we missed a patch of pudding, etc., they could slip or so could we.

We found other ways to add such joy in their lives. I'll talk about them at a later point.

SOME RANDOM THOUGHTS AND A "HAPPY, HAPPY, HAPPY" ENDING FOR 1989 SCHOOL YEAR

For people who have no language and no way to produce it through augmented communication devices, the best way to get to know them is by observation.

Many details can be gleaned by closely observing those who can't communicate in words or even by signing or writing. They have only actions to show you when they're in pain, confused, over-stimulated, angry, hungry, too cold, too hot, or bored.

Closely observing my students taught me the importance of doing so. I could predict seizures and aggression and was beginning to learn about other discomforts. Esther, the elderly woman I cared for at night, was a major part of my learning about this. Unlike most of my students, she could tell me when a discomfort needed attention.

But when seeing a new or odd behavior from a student, my helpers and I would look for a cause. We usually found one: a sliver or sticker in a shoe, a pin or other fastener pinching or poking, a helmet or brace on too tight. All of these and more were discovered by observing and "knowing" our kids.

After my 10-year absence from the classroom, I had to re-learn this, but it came back quickly, given the number of runners and unpredictable students in our room.

Weighing the good days and bad days of my classroom experiences revealed the reason for all my stresses while there. The good days are so few that they

Barbra Badger

stand out clearly. And yet it took many bad days—or at least frustrating ones—to get to a really good one.

This is one of my best days ever.

In 1989 I had a sweet girl who was blind and didn't have many words, but she did talk—mostly parroting. Her mother had several children and was very irresponsible. She and the children lived with her mother. I will call this student Abigail.

Given that I had more students than I could manage, and at the same time traveling to the university several nights a week, then having homework to befittingly suit someone in a master's program, I didn't have much free time to spend doing anything outside those duties.

Abigail needed a new wheelchair because she also had cerebral palsy. She had not only outgrown her old chair, but it had been left outside when she wasn't in it at home. Six or more stair-step children before her and the household's minimal income meant no room in the small house for her chair. It was a disaster.

I asked the Occupational Therapist how we could get her a new one. Everything was signed and already sent to Medi-Cal; all they needed was a sticker that came in the mail to her mother every month for Abigail's needs—be it adaptive spoons or anything up to and including her chair or a special bed.

When I heard that, I began to send notes home, telling the mother how simple it would be to get the new chair. No response for weeks.

Somehow, I got word that Abigail's mom was in the hospital having another baby, so I went there to confirm her home address and get directions so I could get a Medi-Cal sticker from Abigail's grandma.

Occupational Therapy had to re-measure the dimensions on the paperwork because Abigail had grown enough in the interim to require it. I was looking over their shoulder and noticed they had chosen a black one. I frowned and shook my head. We all looked at each other; I pointed to pink and without a word they changed it.

The afternoon I went to the grandmother's, it was raining buckets. I was on my way to class at the university and determined to get that sticker.

Abigail's chair came in May. No longer did we wince when we had to wedge her hips into the too-small space. No longer did we have to deal with rust and ragged upholstery. (When there was time throughout my teaching career, we did clean the chairs when they needed it. I kept Allen wrenches around to repair and tighten any loose parts and WD-40 to loosen stiff ones.)

We put Abigail in her brand new chair and leaned her backward to rest her back. She didn't know it was pink, but as a pretty little girl in a clean, new throne, the rest of the world could see her as a princess.

We were all waiting in the big lobby for the buses to come and be loaded, and in all the hustle and bustle, I saw her lips moving. No one was near enough to be talking to her, so she wasn't parroting. I leaned down to hear what she was saying and couldn't believe my ears.

"Happy. Happy. Happy." She was saying—over and over. Me too, although the tears in my eyes might have cast doubt they were happy, happy, happy tears. It was my last year there. I left the classroom at that point, as I had my master's degree under my belt, and no longer had a reason to stay so far from my husband and home.

As a footnote, when I returned to teaching 10 years later, one of my male assistants came from a classroom where Abigail had been attending. I got an update as to her progress and confirmation that she was her sweet self.

LOCAL-ARC: WORKING WITH DEVELOPMENTALLY DISABLED ADULTS 1989-1994

LOCAL-ARC was a local organization for disabled people and served teens and adults in several different programs. They had placed an ad for a Daily Living Instructor in the local newspaper. The pay was hourly and there were no benefits.

A Bahai family had a lot to do with establishing the organization and were active on the state and local level in the co-coordinating council. Since I am a Bahai, and they knew I needed a job, they suggested I apply.

The last three letters stand for Association for Retarded Citizens. That nomenclature has been changed to eliminate the "R" word from such groups.

It was a pleasant afternoon when I interviewed. The site was a former doctor's office, with a reception area, several smallish side rooms, a kitchen, two bathrooms, and two outbuildings. In a few years we would be using all available space to serve our clients.

The executive director was a lovely, soft-spoken woman with two children at home. Her delight at having someone as qualified as me who was willing to take such a drastic pay cut bubbled out throughout the interview.

Thoughts of meeting an Executive Director had given me visions of a super-efficient, no-nonsense, ambitious woman with little time to spare for underlings such as me. Doreen was all the opposites. She showed no signs of the burdens her position placed on her and nothing but patience for all interruptions and non-working pens and all else that can cause frustration.

My announcement at having secured the position of Instructional Coach, for a few notches above minimum wage, did not impress my husband. In fact, he became so angry that he didn't get over it until we left the area over a decade later. But I knew I could do a good enough job and quickly rise in the ranks of available positions.

It took only a matter of months before a Vocational Coordinator position opened up. When I was hired, that job was held by someone who had no idea what it was or could be. The current coordinator had to learn the meaning of it on the job—and also didn't know that I had a master's in the field of working with this population.

VOCATIONAL CLIENTS

Wes:

If you have a stereotype of handicapped workers as plodding, too-friendly people who use public transportation or ride in the agency van—forget it. Wes held three part-time jobs at one time, and two of those he landed himself after I secured the first one.

He bought himself a new bike with all kinds of extras—a radio, lights, streamers—and rode all over town. One night his fellow workers (not disabled) at his late-night job stole his radio, and a few days after that someone stole the bike.

He didn't talk very much—or very clearly when he did speak. But he had a live-in girlfriend, and they managed to keep up with their bills. Wes was a go-getter and with intense training could hold a job that paid higher than minimum wage.

Most of our clients were upstanding citizens, and one became an advocate at the state level. There were former clients who were alcoholics, streetwalkers, various kinds of addicts, and shoplifters. Only if they accepted the advice of case managers or friends would they ever seek psychological help with these issues. Be that as it may, the law itself is very frustrating. When clients are making bad decisions, no one can stop them unless it is blatant law breaking such as drug dealing or theft that caseworkers become aware of or any other offense where law enforcement must be called.

"What is the worst that can happen?"

Spoiler alert! Tragic story coming up.

A Special Calling ...

Carlos:

Carlos always wore a white shirt and tie. He rode his bike everywhere and had seemingly infinite energy. He wasn't 'hyper', just truly energetic. We knew we could find him a good job, and he would do well if it was a good match and a good job trainer was provided.

He had a severe seizure disorder, and it was vital for him to take his medications as prescribed, on time without missing any. It seems he may have had several meds, plus a shunt. Since he rode his bike everywhere, that made it all the more important that he avoided seizures.

His story is complicated in a unique way. There is a conundrum built into the ethics at the core of the system which serves this population. It has to do with freedom and civil rights.

It took many parent groups many years to get laws written to protect the 'rights' of this population. On the plus side, the DD clientele have the right to vote, drive, marry, live independently, have children, have private bank accounts, and in general make their own life decisions.

On the other hand, these rights apply to some persons who have no ability to make wise, informed, decisions or the ability to extrapolate the outcome of a bad one. They get into financial trouble, drugs, alcohol, and abusive situations and get taken advantage of over and over. OK, so we all do in certain times of our lives, but these folks don't have a hope of gaining the cognitive skills to avoid or extract themselves from life's snarls and snares.

Case in point, Carlos.

When he aged out of high school at 21, he automatically became responsible for his life and future— boom! —overnight. This is true of all clients with developmental disabilities. They still have regional center representatives and those reps may spend a lot of time in court assisting their client to comprehend what is happening but can DO nothing to effect the adult client's decisions.

A Special Calling ...

He was short, and cute and his energy was magnetic. You would see him in his white shirt and tie, riding his bike as though he had lots of places to go and people to meet. He drew people to him. Polite and courteous were also adjectives you heard people use to describe him.

Enter the couple in his peer group who wanted to adopt a child. Zac and Shirley had been trying for a long time to adopt but and were not considered viable candidates.

When Carlos was too old for high school, he also aged- out of the group home he had lived in for some time. Since he was able to make decisions for himself and communicate them, what*ever* he chose to do had to be okay, according to the law.

Zac and Shirley wanted to "'adopt' adopt" him. Because he was an adult and would have been considered as such since age 18, the decision was his. If he wanted to live with this couple, no one could stop him.

The main purpose for him being in a group home was to be certain he took his meds at all the right times. Otherwise, he was good at keeping himself and his room clean, doing his own laundry, making simple, nutritious food, and getting around town without getting lost. Carlos was very capable. Just not reliable with meds since time would get away from him.

He chose to move in with Zac and Shirley. The three of them were very happy with the arrangement. It seemed to be working well for a few months. Then Carlos began to lose energy, seem confused, and became disheveled.

We all got very worried and called his case worker from the regional center.

Nothing could be done except to drill Zac and Shirley on the importance of giving him his meds. We knew they were not responsible enough to be able to do that. Zac could drive and didn't have wrecks, but he chose to disconnect from LOCAL-ARC's services, and he and Shirley were always in financial trouble, with no instructor to help.

There was no one in proximity to keep an eye on all the clients without violating their privacy rights. He lived with them for a couple of weeks. We noticed his energy was waning and he seemed confused.

When we brought this to Carlos' attention, we convinced him to move in with Jerry, another client, and his extended family with older adults.

It was too late.

Carlos was only there a week when Jerry came to work one day without him. The crew supervisor queried. Jerry replied, "I don't know. He was just lying on the floor and wouldn't get up."

The crew supervisor went to the house and looked in the bedroom window. Carlos had seizured in the night and fallen out of bed. The seizure was severe and caused him to stop breathing. When the supervisor looked in the window, Carlos had been dead several hours and was in rigor.

Carlos' death was the most senseless loss I could imagine. I was furious with the system that would allow the situation in the first place. It would allow our clientele to become drug addicts, alcoholics, prostitutes, or homeless through their own ignorance, by virtue of choice. It would not allow any patronizing or saving through intervention on anyone's part -- unless the client sought it.

We anticipated certain clients with Down's syndrome who also had heart involvement to die young or soon after turning 30. We knew of individuals, like Freddie in his 60's who had lymphoma, and others with life-threatening conditions, but Carlos, so full of promise, energy, hope, and ambition, could have lived to a ripe old age and been a contributor to society.

At this writing I have no idea if that ridiculous legislation still exists in such an extreme form.

Granted, there are some persons in the range of such disabilities who can and do learn from their mistakes. They are the ones the legislation serves. For those who cannot learn from said mistakes, life lessons are too complicated to train through repetition. Besides, how many overdoses can someone survive before they're trained not to do it anymore?

After thinking about it, freedom to blow it, and having a

society that's loose with freedom should have taught us—humanity—by now that that much freedom is not a good thing.

Carlos, your example brings home the concept of what constitutes too much choice. It also provides an opportunity to ponder the balance that allows us to explore and learn where the boundaries lie. I'm sorry I didn't get a chance to say good-bye.

Time for more success stories.

Yvonne and Carol:

Yvonne:

Yvonne was one of the first of our clientele to be employed by a national franchise which was not in the food industry. Her employment sparked a movement throughout that franchise to hire others with mild disabilities.

She dusted shelves, unpacked stock, put labels on items, and served as interpreter with her bilingual skills. Many persons labeled "retarded" are bilingual. Are you? I'm not.

An even more impressive fact is that Yvonne qualified as a senior citizen at the time of her hire, and she continued in her job until her knees gave out from dusting the bottom shelves.

Carol:

Was best friends with Yvonne and served as a board member on the local ARC. She also led the way to get other clients to register to vote and worked on a campaign for a local mayoral candidate. Carol participated in state and national conferences for rights for the disabled. She was truly a model representative for the organization. When I met her she was also a senior citizen, managing her finances, keeping a clean house, and helping others with bus schedules and shopping.

Kenny and Freddie:

Kenny:

A few clients had completely normal looks, and some caseworkers had a hard time believing they were disabled at all. Kenny was strong in physique, handsome, soft spoken, and kind in manner. He had a memory that was very short term, which some caseworkers could assume was faked. He landed a job in an area that paid very well, and he did well financially—until he met a woman just a bit smarter but emotionally needy and immature. It was sad to watch his success decline as the relationship got more complex.

Freddie:

One of the kindest—and also nearly the oldest—of our clients was a tall gentleman who would work on any crew on which we needed him. He lived alone until another client was in need of a place, and he graciously took him in because we asked him to.

He had a three-wheeled bike with a large basket, lived alone, did his own shopping, and paid his bills regularly. He was never in any kind of trouble. Only after he acquired a roommate did his life become complicated.

The roommate, Martin, had a reputation for having a temper. His situation was even more complicated by the fact that his mother was a board member who eventually became the executive director.

Freddie had a little dog. He'd had it long enough to determine that he could care for an animal and the animal would be fine. One day he came home from work to find the little dog on his bed, lifeless. Assumptions were made that the roommate had "flipped out" and accidentally killed the dog. Martin denied it the hundred or so times he was asked.

A Special Calling ...

We couldn't be sure, so we moved the roommate.

Freddie didn't get any more pets. He had lymphoma, was in his early 60s, and didn't want his pet to become someone else's responsibility when he died. He did have a girlfriend and they went places together and kept company for a few years. It was an innocent relationship and good for both of them to have a companion for dinner and movies.

Martin's mother did become Executive Director but stayed only a few years. Her husband was in a small plane when it crashed into the ocean. Her husband's funeral and Freddie's were on the same day and at almost the same time. We didn't tell her until long after in order to spare her double the grief.

Freddie's death came at a time when I was being laid off, another friend was diagnosed with terminal cancer, and I developed Graves' disease—that was the diagnosis—but it was a state of shock. Because on top of everything else, my husband was laid off at the same time.

Donny:

Donny had Down's syndrome, although when he dressed up, you couldn't tell unless he spoke. He was on the grounds crew with Freddie and Jerry. The three of them were the "founding" grounds crew. Donny moved somewhat slowly, but he came to work by way of bike. He wore a flak jacket every day and was a familiar figure around town, hunched over the handlebars, the army-green jacket covering his wide shoulders as he rode along at a moderate speed.

Donny was very quiet, perhaps because the Down's speech drew attention to the malady and away from his person.

I know we had many interactions, but there are a few that are tattooed into my memory.

Donny and several other clients lived in a supported-living complex that had a rec room. One Thanksgiving, Carol and the manager of the complex organized a Thanksgiving dinner there.

When I came in, Donny was playing pool, wearing a crisp white shirt and black dress pants.

I didn't recognize him at first. He was very handsome—even debonair. He caught that, because he smiled at me in a way that I could tell he had seen my surprise.

We chatted before lunch, and he was much more at ease than usual. He spoke freely and somewhat clearly. I don't recall what we talked about—or much else about that day—but it put Donny in a different light in my mind.

Even though I am a trained professional, when I hear a label such as Down's syndrome, or CP, or Autistic, my mind has a tendency to make some assumptions about limitations on that person until I see that person and can adjust accordingly. Because any of these issues can be mild, moderate or severe.

None of the above categories or labels can in any way be formed into a cookie cutter typing mechanism.

Donny was beginning to defy my projected limitations on him. It didn't stop there.

The space in the pigeon hole I put him in began to stretch. That resulted in me holding him more accountable for his actions.

One day as the grounds crew was unloading the truck, I happened to see a large bulge in Donny's jacket pocket and asked him what that was. He pulled it out and I went ballistic on him in front of his peers.

It looked to me like a bottle of beer or malt in a fancy-labeled, wide-mouth container. I didn't read the label—I jumped to conclusions and read him the riot act. He rode away on his bike without a word.

The client that had given him the drink waited for me to calm down and informed me it was empty and was not even alcohol. I felt very ashamed for so many reasons. I gave Donny credit for being smarter and more normal now because he had opened up in a comfortable environment. He hadn't really become any smarter than usual, and his friends who did drink wouldn't give him alcohol. I had castigated him in front of his co-workers, peers, and neighbors, and I owed him a public apology.

As I mentioned, many of our clients lived in the same complex. Zac and Shirley, Carol, Yvonne, Donny, and several others were neighbors. I went to Donny's house and apologized right away. The next morning when the crew was loading the truck, I apologized again in front of all of them.

Occasionally, a crew supervisor was absent. In that case I went out with them as supervisor. On one such occasion, Donny and I were unloading the truck at one of the sites, and somehow, I acquired a small but deep gouge on my wrist at the base of my right thumb.

I looked up at him, scowling accusingly. He looked back, puzzled. We stood locked in a wordless loop of misunderstanding. The scar I acquired—I could have gouged myself in my fever to get to work—is shaped like a quarter-inch-wide butterfly. Every time I see it, I see Donny's face looking at me, puzzled, innocent, unaware of the cause of my accusing gaze.

However, I don't need any such reminder of him. There is yet another reason he is memorable.

Our efforts at getting local businesses to employ our clients was ongoing, and new businesses were an excellent resource. A new restaurant contacted us before we called them, which really raised our spirits.

I answered the phone. "This is Barbra, Vocational Coordinator."

Donny was standing in the doorway of my office.

Man on phone: "We are opening a restaurant in a few weeks, around Thanksgiving, and we want to have a Santa here for Christmas. Do you have anyone who would like to do that? They could give the kids some candy and we'll have someone to take Polaroids with Santa. Does that sound like something your folks could do?"

Me: "You want a Santa! What a great idea. A Santa!"

I looked over at Donny to share my enthusiasm, never thinking he would be interested. He was so shy.

Donny nodded, pointed to himself, and lisped, "I want to be Santa."

Me: "I have a volunteer standing right here. You have a Santa. How long would you want him, and do you have a suit or should we find one?"

I honestly don't remember the rest of the phone conversation, but a board member had a Santa suit complete with a red velvet bag and Donny and I went hunting for candy to give to the children.

We found a store with a plethora of candy. We looked up and down long rows of Christmas confections and pondered the practicality of each one. There were some very small candy canes individually wrapped. "Too small," he said. There were bags of specially wrapped "Kisses" and "Hugs" and an endless collection of chocolates of varying sizes. "Too messy," he said.

Near the end of this infinite collection, something caught his eye: rows of bright yellow candy canes with rainbow stripes in a box declaring, "Cherry-flavored, rainbow-colored candy canes."

We grabbed several boxes. He took them home, took them out of the box, and placed them in a Santa bag. We got him a wig—he didn't need a pillow and he looked great. He was Hispanic, and the white beard and trim on the suit emphasized his dark skin.

Donny now had two jobs: grounds crew during the day and Santa from Friday evening to Sunday evening. He loved it. He was good at it. He was a gentle, quiet Santa. Many times, the exuberant "HO HO HOs " are off-putting to the children, even scary. Donny sat quietly while the parents led the children to him, and he gently held them until they wanted down or the polaroid picture was formed.

The board members of the association gave a Christmas party each year and Donny was Santa then too.

Freddie was there, dressed as a six-foot Christmas tree for a skit, and he looked very tired after the party. It was later than usual for him to be out.

We were closed for the Holidays, so a phone call early

in morning the day after Christmas was unexpected.

"Hello?"

It was the grounds crew supervisor. "You will never guess who died!"

"Freddie?"

"No. Donny. He died on Christmas Day." She stopped to sob. "He had a heart attack."

A vital detail about Donny, undiscovered by me, was that he had the heart condition that some persons with Down's have. I had seen his collection of special Olympic medals, which was more than I thought possible to acquire. He had gotten them for running. It never occurred to me he would have the heart issue

Thinking back over the past few weeks. Donny had kept telling us his chest hurt. We assumed he was getting bored with his work. When the Santa job came along, he stopped mentioning his chest.

The next day we all went back to work and arranged to have a memorial for him in the rec room of the complex. When I went to the manager to secure the room, she informed me that Donny's mother was in his apartment and I could tell her of our plans. In times when our hearts are open, they are as open to acquaintances as they are to family and friends. Our hearts were open to each other in our sadness.

We sat on the couch, holding hands.

"We always knew he would pass ahead of me," his mother said, "but it was so sudden and …"

I waited a moment then added,

"There was no time to say goodbye." And we hugged and wept together.

Santa Donny was the only person to pass away in that town on Christmas Day that year.

It rained off and on from the time Donny passed until well after the memorial service. On New Year's Day my husband and I took a drive—we went looking for the sunshine.

My thoughts were of Donny as we ascended a hillside and the clouds dissipated, spreading themselves thin enough to see through. It was still sprinkling lightly, but we could see the sunshine was just around the next bend.

When we rounded the curve, on my right was the arch of a lovely rainbow. I could see both ends of it! We drove around and past it. It was as though it had been placed there with purpose as we passed from a week of rain to the sun.

For several years after, even after leaving ARC and going back into the classroom, I gave my students' caregivers a note about Donny at Christmas, attached to Cherry-Flavored, Rainbow-Colored Candy Canes in memory of Donny, the best Santa I ever knew.

> My husband reminded me: Donny languished in the ER for 5 hours before being seen. My husband is still angry about it.

Mike:

When I was not fast enough to get jobs for our clients, some would get their own through sheer persistence. From time to time construction projects took place on the main thoroughfare.

Mike a slender, capable fellow would stand by for days and watch. Little by little he stepped in to collect pieces of wood left lying about. Then one of the workmen who didn't realize he was not 'hired' would give him a different task. He would carry it out quickly and efficiently and wait for another. This went on for a week or so and the supervisor hired him.

Mike is an example of two things that frequently happen when our clientele goes to work. Mike and some of his friends rented furniture, appliances, and electronics from a Rent-to-Own place. Inevitably they would fall behind in payments and the things they rented were unusable from disuse and neglect.

The salesmen would be happy to see them coming in

and very unhappy when the bills were overdue and the items unusable for anyone else.

The second thing that happened over and over was the disruption of SSI, their monthly payment from social security.

If they didn't report their new income to SSI, it would go on for a while before SSI became aware. Meanwhile, their disability payment would come at the same amount. When SSI discovered this, the client would have to repay 'over payments'. The idea being when they work their SSI would be reduced by the amount of their work pay.

Eventually they would be off SSI and bring in even more through their work.

While I was the vocational coordinator, several clients got jobs that paid minimum wage and more, but always without exception, panicked and quit as soon as SSI dinged them for overpayment. They couldn't understand the relationship between the increase in outside income and the reduction of SSI. They didn't want SSI to shrink or disappear for any reason.

Mike went through these cycles several times. He would find his own work, rent several items, lose some SSI, quit his job and struggle through the time it took to repay the overpayment.

It was also clear that the personnel at Social Security office did not understand how much our clients did NOT understand.

POSITIVE MEMORY

A local community college allowed me to organize a non-credit class for my clientele. Some of them could read and some could hold a blue-collar job. We spent our time discussing what they would like to explore at the college, and they went about signing up for non-credit cooking classes or craft classes, and one even became a nurses' aide. I really enjoyed that whole process. When we left the area a few years later, the class was still in effect.

My timelines are blurred as to when I left ARC and went to work for Catholic Charities, but it was another blow to my husband when I made that decision. It was another non-profit and something I loved doing. He felt stuck in work he was not enjoying, and he saw my choices as being under-employed and not using the degree we had both sacrificed to achieve. True enough, but I was still not ready to return to the classroom.

There are memorable stories from working at Catholic Charities, some uplifting and some that are not, but they don't belong here in my teaching years group of essays.

BACK TO THE CLASSROOM: 1998-99 SCHOOL YEAR – A 10 YEAR BREAK

The first interview that put me in the classroom—back in 1987—had a few glitches, but the principal wanted someone around the age of her most difficult parents—so tag, I was it.

My next interview, this one more successful, was in 1998. I remember the exact moment that one of the five principals at the table chose me. After I boasted about how I had dealt with my most difficult runner—the boy with pica we trained to pick up litter—one of the principals made some side remark to another teacher that, "I'd like to see how that would work with XXXX." She hired me.

My childhood wish to be a teacher, and my rose-colored thoughts of, *When I get my own classroom, things will be different,* were no longer what I was thinking when I returned to the classroom. Having what I thought to be the most difficult student, or having seen some others, partially prepared me for this room of high school-aged and adult-sized, mostly boys.

However, I did imagine perhaps something magical or meaningful would occur when I first opened the door to my room. It didn't. So much for expectations.

Yet, for several reasons that door was the cause of a stressful beginning to this classroom.

SPLIT-SECOND TIMING

"Maintaining a safe environment" is teacher-speak—and critical—when dealing with highly unpredictable people. As a teacher of severely autistic high school students, safety was constantly on my mind, and I tried to be at least three steps ahead of my students. One in particular, Wayne. Because my students were non-verbal, mind reading was essential. Thanks to Wayne, planning for contingencies to prevent disaster among severely autistic kids became one of my strengths.

But our first year together he had a lot to teach me. In many ways Wayne was the sharpest of my students that year. He could learn how to put something together by watching someone else take it apart. He would bide his time and watch for opportunities to escape from the group, inside or out. These and other talents made him a danger to himself. He had an ugly burn scar on his thigh that he caused by mixing bleach and ammonia and then spilling it on his leg. If given the opportunity, he would stab himself, or cut himself with scissors. But his favorite death defying feat was to run out into heavy traffic. He was hell-bent on self-destruction. I learned a lot about prevention of disasters by having him in my environment

County Schools had hired me the previous April. I was 52 at the time, and it had been 10 years since I'd used my credentials. Painful memories from my previous classroom experiences returned as soon as I walked through that classroom door.

On a day early in my first complete school year at that high school, I was mentally busy preparing a schedule for the coming week. The disaster plan for my room was due by the end of the school day, and I could barely keep the names of my students straight at that point. Re-learning previous skills, absorbing new information about my students' histories and families, the protocol of the school, the politics, my assistants' abilities, and deadlines to meet were spinning around in my head. Anxiety was my middle name.

My first students to arrive each day, Mark, Johnny, Zeke, Claudio ... and Wayne ... were already in the room, but my first assistant, Eileen, was late, and the next assistant wasn't due for half an hour. I had to go to the parking lot to meet the bus, which was bringing me three more students.

Why do they stagger the arrival times of assistants? I mentally grumbled as I stepped outside, hoping to see Eileen or find someone else willing to help for a minute. My gaze was on the bus driver, who was waiting for someone to come and collect the students. My mind was still spinning as I took two steps forward and then ... The heavy classroom door closed behind me with a distinctive *click*! I'd forgotten to set the lock to the OPEN position and the keys were on my desk. I felt the concrete open up and drop out beneath me, and I was falling into that deep chasm. I turned and furiously pulled on the door, but it was futile.

Oh! No! Oh. My. God. No! Locked out, and all my unpredictable students are locked in with no supervision. Wayne! Mark! Oh my God, what's happening in there? Given my penchant for writing, my imagination created several horrifying scenes. I darted to the window to evaluate the action inside the room. Johnny stood on the other side, grinning back at me, not aware that I couldn't get back in. Zeke stayed on his chair, all six-foot-two of him, rocking, when he could have been chasing the others around the room with his five-foot reach to pull their hair or tear their clothes. Claudio was quiet, but he was prone to frequent and severe seizures which could occur at any time. Wayne was across the room, looking out the bank of windows that made up the back wall. His back was to the door and he was oblivious to the situation ... so far. *Thank God for that.* Had he known, he could have hurt himself badly in a number of ways. Mark paced for a while and then crossed into the kitchen area. I had established a rule a few days before to keep him out of there unless supervised one on one. I knew it would take thousands of reminders for him to learn this rule. Left to himself, he could impulsively empty the contents of drawers and cupboards onto the floor in search of favored snacks, and then Wayne could reap the benefits of scissors and knives "falling from heaven," which Mark may have dislodged from hidden places. My mind worked on how to prevent such a disaster in the future, while I paced and looked for help. The room was somewhat isolated. Cell phones were just beginning to make their way into the work place, and the only walkie-talkies were in the hands of the security guards. Time would bring a solution, but this had happened in a split second ... and so could untold numbers of harmful incidents inside that room.

The bus driver brought me the students since she had to make other stops. Another embarrassment. I prided myself in being able to do it all. You know, a "bring home the bacon and cook it up in a pan" type thing. Now I had five students inside and three outside and no help. Two of the students outside also had seizure conditions. One student was a "wanderer" and one was in a wheelchair. The third student was calm and complacent, but they all had to be toileted after their long bus ride. Eileen finally appeared, apologizing and at first not quite understanding what was happening. She had gone through the Special Ed system as a student and had become an instructional assistant 17 years before. She was caring and knew all the kids in the severe- and profound-designated classes. However, ability to deduce, infer, and long-term recall had to be done by someone else.

Eileen took the wanderer with her to find a security guard or janitor with a key to open the door. Meanwhile, inside, Wayne was still standing across the room with his back to the front windows. I was pleading with him to come open the door, something he was fully capable of and more than happy to do at any other time as an accomplished escapee. Mark stopped pacing and started emptying the cupboards containing snacks. Johnny toddled to the kitchen area and laughed while Mark—pardon my sarcasm—for the first time ever completed a task. Johnny was smart enough to know that was a big taboo and any broken taboo made him laugh gleefully every time.

Eileen returned with Manny. He didn't have a key, but he came with tools to take the door off its hinges, and he deftly went to work. Manny did double duty as a security guard and the girls' softball coach; he had also chased down and captured Wayne many times during the previous two years. Eileen and I used our best "Mom" voices to try to get Johnny or Wayne to open the door ... slowly. Wayne finally came to the window and looked out to where all the adults and half of his class were standing. Confusion flashed on his face ... a very bad sign. When he got a confused look, he would usually "go off" and run as if his life were at stake. *If he hits that door while Manny is working on it, no one can stop it from crushing Manny and maybe Wayne.* I increased efforts to sooth and coax Wayne to calmly open the door. However, he ran back across the room. Wayne would spend most of his days trying to get out when he was to be in—but not now. Outside, Manny kept up a commentary on his progress, assuring everyone that the ordeal was in capable hands and might soon be over. Inside, Wayne finally noticed Manny's voice and moved closer. "I've got the bottom post loosened," Manny said, "but I won't take it out until Wayne is on the other side of the room so he doesn't just bolt out and knock us all over." My reply carried more panic than I intended to show. "He's in the middle of the room now, Manny, and could go in any direction."

Eileen called to Johnny to open the door, while at the same time watching the seizure-prone students—inside the room and outside. Our "knight to the rescue" pulled out another post. First, Wayne began flapping his arms then suddenly, Mark dumped the silverware drawer. Wayne's flapping increased, and he ran back to the opposite side of the room. Tension was escalating inside. There was at least one pair of scissors on the floor. Manny heard the clatter.

"Where is he now, I'm about to pull the third post?" "He's pacing in the kitchen area—flapping!"

Since he was flapping, he was less likely to notice the scissors, but Manny knew flapping meant time was getting short for him to finish before Wayne would hit the door, running full bore. The door was two inches thick—solid metal—and even Manny would hesitate to try to catch it if it were falling on him. "If Wayne or Johnny come and open it," Manny said, "even if there's only one post out of the four, if they open it gently, the weight of the door will probably keep it in place. I'll leave the top one in then it can't fall all the way out. If it did, it might twist the hinge out of alignment. But this big door won't fall on anyone—at least I hope not."

"Wayne knows you. Would you try?" I asked. "He hasn't responded to Eileen or me at all."

Manny called for him, "Wayne! Come open the door, buddy! I'll take you for a walk."

Manny had a soft but manly voice and the patience of a saint. All of our guys liked Manny. Johnny went to Wayne, tapped him on the shoulder, and pointed to our side of the room. Wayne looked a little startled but stopped flapping and walked toward the door. The angle of view made it impossible to see him once he was within three feet of the door. No one could see his body language or facial expression. He could have stopped to sit on the floor, or have been grabbed by Zeke, or be getting ready to make a full-blast run for it.

Manny continued the mantra, "Open the door, Wayne. I'll take you for a walk,". I stared at the hinges. Except for one meager post, the heavy door was now free to stray in any direction at the slightest imbalance. The door moved. Wayne opened the door slowly and held it until Eileen took over. "Thank you, Wayne. You're such a gentleman!" said Eileen. "Now go to the bathroom before you go with Manny." She held the hands of two students, one on each side, as she swept through the doorway. Manny put the posts back in while Wayne complied with Eileen's suggestion and everything settled down again.

A Special Calling ...

     Wayne's smile at Manny, his purring sound when they started down the walkway, was notable. Manny talked to him like they were old friends and handed him the walkie-talkie. Wayne's face lit up like 100-watt bulb. I made a mental note, *Wayne likes electronic objects*. The rest of the year was a lot like that—with a different set of stresses each day—but I never had a locked-door incident again.

RUNNERS AT THE HIGH SCHOOL LEVEL

Wayne had psychotic behaviors. However, due to the extent of his developmental level and lack of speech, there was no way to diagnose him, and my credibility with psych personnel was close to nil. In addition to the psychotic tendencies, as I mentioned previously, he was self-destructive.

When he did escape the room, sometimes his main goal seemed to be to run down the middle of the road, enticing traffic to run over him.

Even though Wayne had no speech, he made his own sounds that escalated in intensity when he was getting upset. He made "flying" motions with his arms that accompanied his "get me outta here" sounds and behavior, and the expression on his face and in his eyes were of pure horror and panic.

If psychiatrists had had the time to observe him as much as we did, they would have been fascinated, I am certain, and hopefully, may have tried to find a way to diagnose and treat him. Wayne would stand by the windows, softly making his sounds or merely pacing slowly, eventually becoming agitated, and then suddenly, with a look of utter horror on his face, flap wildly and bust out through the door.

I am convinced he was hearing voices or hallucinating that the whole place was on fire. His efforts to escape were on the level of primal self-preservation, not just an "I am going to leave the room no matter what you do" action. It took two helpers and me to hold him back. We also put up a large foam wedge to block the door. Wayne had been in a group home for several years and was two years from aging out of my room when I was hired as his teacher. My principal and her husband had Wayne in their own classrooms as teachers and knew full well what I was up against.

One day he ran across campus and up to the second floor of a building, darted into the journalism class, and disappeared in the company of his peers. That was a good day. Manny brought him back.

In addition to being a runner, Wayne liked to pull fire alarms. We had a hideously noisy one in our room disconnected because it didn't alarm anywhere but in our room with our severely autistic and seizure-prone kids. I glued it shut as soon as I discovered no one could hear it but us and no signal was sent to any fire station.

The first time I took Wayne for a walk around the campus, he showed me how much more he knew about it than I did. He was very calm and serene for the whole walk, which seemed to belie all that I had been told about him. He stayed beside me in silence.

Even when we entered the back door of the main office, he didn't give any indication of what he was about to do. The secretary had her back to us, and there was a coach at the teachers' mailboxes. As we entered, a door directly across from us was standing full open with a wall of wires and lights and buttons exposed.

Wayne took four giant steps, went straight to it, and pulled the main fire alarm for the entire school.

I have no idea how he knew what lever to pull; it wasn't obvious to me.

I was mortified, mystified, and stood in stunned disbelief while the secretary stabbed me with her steely looks. County classrooms—those that deal with the most special of Special Ed students—are not highly regarded by the regular education circles. The whole school experienced an unscheduled fire drill, and the secretary had to call all the fire station and explain it was a false alarm. The school had to pay some fee because of it.

I never took him near the office again, and I always stressed the importance for whoever walked with him to stay between him and any of the outside alarms. No other false alarm was his doing for the remainder of his high school terms. Yes, I am boasting. I'll take any form of success I can eke out.

During his last week of school, several times a day he ran to the farthest gates and tried to squeeze out between the five-inch spaces. He also refused to get on or off the bus without full-on physical "assistance." I would learn that his passiveness, though frustrating, was better than the full-on aggressiveness I would experience with future students.

Few things could bring him back from a distance run. What might work one time would not work another time. If he came back for me one day, he would only come back for a different person another day. If he came back for a soda on Monday, he wouldn't on Tuesday or Wednesday.

Bus transitions were very predictable. He would always resist getting on or off the bus. It was never a simple, easy process. Our days started and ended fighting with Wayne, cajoling him, pleading, enticing, eventually dragging or carrying him on or off the bus. If we promised a "reward" for his compliance, he would take the reward and immediately reverse his behavior. As soon as the reward—usually an M&M—was ingested, he would fall to the floor of the bus or ground and refuse to get up. I never told myself, "This is just how it is." I couldn't accept that I just hadn't found the right words, or tone, or combination that would work. His behavior, his success at thwarting us, had to be my ineptitude. Some small voice inside me is still telling me that.

Be that as it may, I made a habit of observing my students in as many environments as possible. I would stand back and watch their interactions with others, what they did when they thought no one was looking, what seemed to draw their attention—or even hold it—and what foods they liked/disliked. I would sit next to them, exploring every nuance of expression, studying their souls.

One of my strengths was understanding my students and seeing small changes that might mean something.

Wayne liked to put flashlights together. He did so with no errors the first time we showed him how. All the way down to turning it on and checking to see if it worked. We had several repetitive assembly work tasks for our students. Wayne was good at all of them, and we had nothing beyond the flashlight—a six-step process—to challenge him. True to his peerage, he had senioritis and would only do a few flashlights before leaving the work area. The IEP goal was to stay at the task for 30 minutes but nothing could keep him there.

This is a good place to mention one of the crazy-making things that has always plagued me. Regardless of what level any student functions, once they show they can function at a level higher than suspected, I get indescribably frustrated when that student refuses to apply their skills. I learned that about myself when I was an instructional assistant in the learning-disabled class. The students had many capacities they refused to use. I wound up screaming at their passive-aggressiveness and never did learn how to deal effectively with their attitude or my frustration with it.

One day Wayne began screaming like never before and curled up in a ball on the floor. I called the Behavior Specialist and let him hear the screams. When he arrived, he checked Wayne for a hernia or tenderness in his abdomen indicating inflamed appendix. He found nothing. Then he had Wayne do some of the tasks he was required to do by his IEP goals. Wayne performed them expertly with no resistance. It seems our behaviorist was the only man in Wayne's life. All group home attendants were female, my aide and I were female, and although his bus driver was male, Wayne didn't comply with his efforts either. But for this man he was an angel.

He never screamed that way again, and we never did figure out why he had done it at all.

The day of his graduation he was very subdued and seemed to sense the meaning and grasp the zeitgeist of the day. He looked very handsome in his white shirt and tie and made no attempts to run that day. I decorated the room with tissue-paper flowers I had been making all year after school as therapy. There were nearly a hundred of them, and they were all between five and seven inches wide.

I made a nice poster with Wayne's picture on it, in addition to the flowers, but this was my first graduation party. More elaborate décor embellished the room for future grads.

I have longer stories about the more difficult students because I had to spend more one-on-one time with them, and observing them in order to better deal with them.

FOLLOW-UP ON WAYNE

Leaving the school setting puts these kids in strange new worlds. Those in group homes have no more than 8 residents and 4 shifts of helpers to share a space with. In their classrooms, ideally there are no more than 10 with 2 or 3 assistants.

Out in the rest of the world most 'day care' facilities are back to warehousing conditions. Too many clients and too few well-trained workers.

First Wayne went to a place that trained the clients to care for animals. The feeding and watering of chickens, goats and sheep were simple enough duties. When I heard of his placement, I wondered if it was a good idea. Only a few clients at a time went there and it was away from busy streets. Unfortunately, it didn't work out. Wayne had dashed out of the gate and left it open. The ensuing chaos resulted in the animals escaping and the program was literally trashed.

He didn't do well in his next placement either, but that was not his fault. The program who took him in didn't understand the degree of 'runner' I was telling them about, or did not understand my use of the word. The program used their more capable clients to deliver Meals on Wheels. A large van carried some clients from house to house and each client was assigned to take the food to the door. He bolted from the van in the middle of a busy street and when the staff was struggling to get him back in someone called the FBI because they thought he was being kidnapped.

That's all I know of Wayne.

A SILLY STORY

No one is perfect and as hard as I tried and for the most part succeeded in 'maintaining a safe environment' one afternoon was another heart-stopper. Prepping to go home can get a bit confusing especially if our buses and the regular ed kids were occupying the parking lot at the same time with our buses coming and the high school kids raring to go--leaving. It must have been a Friday because that is the most difficult day to control the flow.

Two of our students, one who had shown a preference for male companionship and one who would follow without objection anyone holding his hand left the room unnoticed.

One of the regular ed students came to the door and told us they were walking down the busy street where the high school kids were driving away or we would never known what happened to them until the police contacted their homes.

My fastest runner ran the quarter mile to get them and bring them back where their bus was waiting.

He said they made quite a pair just plodding along oblivious to any danger. The drivers of the cars maneuvering carefully around them.

TRANSFORMATION OF MARK AND ME

It remains a mystery to me why one of my students I found most difficult to cope with is planted firmly in my heart. He was one of the most exasperating students I ever had, especially when we first met. He was in constant motion, and that motion included biting his hand, moaning, screeching, panting, and occasionally seizing. He once had a seizure like I had never seen before. He was sitting on the floor, playing with my keys or something of that nature when he suddenly began screaming in obvious pain and fell backwards. He had never done that before and never did it again.

That boy could have been a poster child for the idea that vaccinations cause mental retardation and autism. His mother reported he was fine and even had some words until he was two. He lost everything, even walking, very quickly after a deluge of booster shots. Research has shown; however, the shots are not to blame in any way. Yet the evidence, as related to coincidence, is strong. The number of incidents as it relates to dates of boosters and quantity of injections is staggering.

Even before he made great strides in his behavior, Mark was a favorite. He became even more endeared to me when, as he matured, his responsiveness and receptivity increased.

Mark was a bane to many teachers before me, but his first teacher shared my warm feelings for him. She and her assistant, who was now *my* assistant, taught Mark to walk when he was six years old. My assistant often remarked that she thought it had been a mistake.

All Mark wanted was to go outside. After he learned to walk, he couldn't be stopped. Even though he was as tall as I was, about five foot, he had the mannerisms and the aura of a toddler. When he scooted out the door, he was just like a toddler taking control of his direction. He wasn't very fast and we easily caught him.

But compared to Wayne, Mark's feats of escaping were comical. He was very impulsive, and most of the time he telegraphed his intentions to leave the room with a very readable impish expression and, most of the time, a squeal of delight. Even if we couldn't see his expression, the squeal would give him away. He did want to leave several times on some days, however, and my first year with Mark gave me lots of exercise. I use Mark as an example of how hard my class was to work with, by giving the example that it took us years to get him to sit—in a chair or in a group setting—for more than 10, 20, or 30 seconds.

When I first observed the class during the student's lunch, an assistant would follow Mark as he paced and popped bits of food in his mouth.

That was wrong on so many levels.

Mark's most nerve-wracking characteristic was his sounds. For the first two years that we occupied the same room, his sounds were constant during his waking hours. They were not ear-splitting, just constant, droning and moaning. They took hours to wear on a person, but wear they did, at least for the first two years.

We learned the way to keep Mark from leaping up and running, either around the room or out the door, was to stand in front of him while he was sitting, and keep our knee touching his knee. Eventually, we didn't have to do that, but it took years.

In the beginning, at various times during the day, we would have him sit on the floor in the eating area for up to 30 seconds at a time. He would be biting his hand and squealing and trying to get up after only a few seconds, but we kept with it, and eventually, he would sit and just moan, not squeal, for the full 30 seconds.

A Special Calling ...

As time went on, we had him sit at the table, out of reach of other students' food, (so he wouldn't grab it and stuff it in his mouth) and let him put finger foods in his own mouth. When he got up after only a few seconds of sitting there, we would sit him back down and he would scream.: stand up-sit down-scream-stand up- sit down scream.

Mark and a few others slept at school, due to the medications they took which cross-wired their sleep habits, keeping them awake all night. Mark's mother was not happy about that, but eventually he began to thrive in the sense of gaining self-control and maturing naturally.

His medications continued to be altered and time went on. One year I had two male assistants. Both were Godsends to me and all my boys. I had Mark for five years. He developed from being in perpetual motion with aimless movement and squealing to gradually sitting quietly for longer and longer periods of time. He went from being fed while in motion to sitting at the table, eating quietly, standing when finished, and walking calmly to sit or lie on one of the couches for a nap.

Most of his progress I owe to one of my assistants who put in the time and patience to help Mark bloom.

This next Mark story is a lesson I needed that didn't come directly from him.

Mark was already doing better about not grabbing other people's food, but I was still very strict about it.

One day after work I took my helpers to a neat little burger stand across the street from the school. We already had our food and were chatting when three boys, high-school aged or just past it, blustered into our quiet confab. Two of the boys went to the counter and ordered food. The other one was a copy of our student, physically with curly hair and blue eyes and facially. He paced and chattered while his two friends went on about business. Then they went to a booth to sit and wait for their food to come—except the clone. He sat on the edge of the table. It was exactly what our guy would do and what we had been trying to change. My helpers and I looked at each other, we were all thinking the same thing.

Mark! A normal Mark! While his friends were sitting there eating their food, and the Mark clone was leaning over, snagging fries here and fries there, no one cared. When they were finished—Mark's twin never did sit down—the other two boys got into the cab of the truck, "Mark" pulled down the tail gate, jumped into the bed and then, on top of the cab, spun around, hopped down, and got into the cab by sliding through the window. The other guys had not paid any attention to him, except to try to open the door and let him in. I learned from that, and from then on, I was a lot more relaxed about Mark's food stealing and not sitting down. Because, truth be known, he was no worse than the boy we had seen the day before.

One day, in his more mature stage, Mark was out with one of my helpers, and the security guards were chasing an errant student from Regular Ed.

I've mentioned that Mark loved to play catch-me-if-you-can, and that usually took place with him slipping out the door, then being caught by us 40 feet away. He would squeal with delight at the game and rub his hands together near his face at his diabolical plan of mischief. His eyebrows would knit in toward each other, adding more impishness to his demeanor. Add in crooked grin and you have the expression of a perfect little devil.

But one day he and my assistant were outside in the wide-open expanse of the campus, and two grown men—security guards—were in full pursuit of a teenager. Mark's eyes lit up like a 500-watt bulb and off he ran toward the miscreant, squealing with delight.

Mark had a better lead on the boy than the men and soon overtook him, trapping him against a fence. The kid seemed terrified of this squealing, obviously not-right-in-the-head guy who was grinning and drooling and standing much too close for comfort. The student froze against the fence, while Mark kept squealing his joy, hoping the boy would run again.

The security guards knew Mark well and were always kind to him. They were laughing uproariously at the terrified kid Mark had cornered, and the kid was probably relieved to be taken into their custody.

Mark laughed and squealed all the way back to the room.

Mark was very loving and would spontaneously grab me around the neck and hug me. He usually left some drool on my face and hair, but he always smiled, those blue eyes peering out from under curly hair.

When Mark aged out—our term for graduation—he had acquired a skill of pushing a large trash barrel around while my assistant or another student put litter in it. That was his only work-oriented skill.

He had another skill that I have not seen equaled. Unfortunately, I know of no work where he could apply it. He could aim at and kick in a straight line any object on the ground in front of him.

It was usually pen caps, bottle tops, or small rocks, but he could also do it with a soccer ball.

As soon as I discovered he could do it with a soccer ball, I took him out to the field when the boys in gym class were playing soccer and let him run in among them. He got some ya-yas out running on the field, and the other boys got to see he had a talent and really wasn't so scary.

Mark's progress could only be attributed to teamwork in and out of the classroom.

My deepest gratitude and thanks to all who played a part.

I mentioned before our grad parties got more elaborate. For his we made a paper Mache head of Shamu popping out of the wall. The rest of the room was beach-themed with beach balls hanging from the ceiling and beach scenery on every blank wall.

ZEKE AND THE "GOOD" YEAR—THEN THE BAD ONES

Zeke was six-two and had a five-foot reach. I've mentioned him before. His mental development was at maybe nine months. He was handsome, and in photos you would never know how delayed he was. His diagnosis was CP. He could walk but had balance issues.

During the good year, I had two male helpers in my class of mostly grown, mostly boys. We had a portable basketball hoop about seven feet high. Zeke got pretty good at it, and his hand-over-hand aim was even better. All of our boys spent at least a half hour a day shooting baskets. If one of the girls wanted to try, they got in on it too.

One of my assistants frequently took Zeke walking, and his balance improved a lot. That activity also cut down on his rocking while sitting in the room.

On quiet afternoons the whole room would brighten up when anyone reached into the fridge and pulled out Popsicles, Zeke's face would beam, he would laugh his own special laugh, and bounce up and down in his chair. He never got up to take a Popsicle from us but waited to be invited to come to the table to eat it.

A Follow-Up A person who worked at Zeke's group home told me about an incident that happened 10 years or so after I left that classroom.

The group home had taken him and some other residents to Disneyland. I was shocked to hear that--but the person reported Zeke had done fine for the whole day--until they were leaving. He grabbed a girls hair and wouldn't let go. "It was bad, very bad." is all he could say due to confidentiality concerns.

I was so relaxed during that year that I told personnel to send me trainees for assistants. The following year, after one of my helpers left, I was so stressed I had completely forgotten I had made that request and yelled at personnel for sending me people who didn't know anything.

Another thing I had forgotten about was how much I wanted to be a teacher so long ago, and all I could remember was that I came back to the classroom, kicking and screaming. That is, until my principal told me she thought "someone who wanted to be a teacher" should be in my place. I said that was me, the one who had wanted to be a teacher all their life. But co-workers only heard me say the "kicking and screaming" part, and confusion reigned over all. This disconnect was not intentional at all, but it was a part of the overall disarray in my personal life.

The following year my other male helper left and I went over the edge.

During this time of stress, one afternoon I went home with a headache and couldn't find anything strong enough to deal with it. There was some Vicodin prescribed for my husband after dental work, so I took that, even though I knew taking any opiate makes me sick to my stomach. I was also quite depressed, enough so that I looked for a number for suicide prevention just for someone to talk to.

There were no other Special Ed teachers near me. My state of mind had caused me to make inappropriate statements, which caused those I worked with to dislike me. I really needed someone to talk to.

The phone book didn't have a suicide prevention number, so I called 911 to see if they had a number. My tongue was loose enough that when they asked if I was having thoughts of suicide, I replied, "Every day of my life."

Bit of advice—Don't ever say that to a 911 operator!

They have a protocol to follow and it goes like this: They are obligated to send a sheriff to your house to evaluate the situation.

The sheriff arrived, looked around, and determined no one else was there nor would there be for several days. He asked me for the bottle of Vicodin and discovered it still contained several pills and, for all those reasons, I was informed he must take me to a hospital for a more thorough evaluation.

Protest all you want, he will cuff you if he has to!

The Vicodin had done its work, and I had thrown up before the sheriff's deputy got there, but I was not feeling any more headache pain.

My district had a procedure to follow when calling for a sub. It was a bit complex, and I needed the paper with the information on it in order to accomplish it. However, given the state of mind I was in, I was lucky to remember my purse.

The deputy drove like a mad man to test my willingness to live or die. I knew what he was doing and didn't play the game. I remained stoic. When we arrived at the hospital, while he talked to a couple of people, I watched the nurses pump someone's stomach. The patient protested loudly and the nurses kept saying, "You've been through this enough times you know it's better just to relax." I could relate. I had made three serious attempts decades before, and this was not anything close to those potential outcomes. This was NOT an attempt on my part.

Several hours went by. Meanwhile, I "sobered" up and was becoming angry because I had no way home. The deputy who brought me was under no obligation to take me back—40 miles—and I had no way to inform my work about my absence should the hospital decide to keep me.

If the psych who evaluated me there found me a bona fide 5150—a danger to myself or others—the hospital would keep me for 72 hours. I had no way to contact my husband or my work, and I knew I wasn't a danger—all I had wanted was someone to talk to. But by the time they got around to talking to me, it was clear they didn't want to hear about my problems.

I was curt with the interviewer, but out of eight people interviewed, I was the only one who got sent home. One couple just needed a cot and three squares, but they were allowed to stay. I had to pay a stranger $50 to take me home.

By that time, it was long after eleven o'clock, and I was exhausted. When I got up after four hours of sleep, I went to work, grateful to have been set free but still in a lot of emotional pain. And that didn't change.

To tell of the major reason for my distress would cause too much anguish for others. I am not a martyr, just considerate.

But suffice it to say, I had caused my husband enough grief, and it would accomplish nothing good to burden anyone else.

However, at that point in my life, those in my field who despised me might not have found me so despicable. All the disturbances have since settled out. Life is now calm and good. But that was not so during the seven years I taught at the high school.

***

One of my students had been with me for three years, and he suddenly began to be violent. He was nearly 18. If he had been a Regular Ed student, he would have been able to drop out and no one could have stopped him.

As he was getting off the bus one morning, I reached up to help him balance coming down the stairs. He grabbed my arm, bit through a suede jacket, and broke the skin.

He wasn't angry or frustrated at the time, so it didn't make sense. He did become angry and frustrated in the following months and years. After being away for so long and developing greater compassion for him, I can only conclude his own arm hurt. That was his only way to tell us.

When his teeth hurt I understood why he kept hitting his jaw. We informed his mother and she took him to the dentist. He stopped hitting his jaw. But I was too far gone at the time he bit me to see through that.

After four years in one room, they moved me and my students to a different high school. He got worse and so did I. We fought the moment he got off the bus, and I had his mother come get him so he wouldn't hurt others.

In the new classroom, they sent me more students with aggressive tendencies. There was little time to focus on goals when everyone was fending off aggressive behaviors. I also had no time to find the "spot" for all of them, which had been the key in the previous classroom.

Assistants went through my room like water. One year, after a hard rain, I saw evidence of a rodent. One assistant had a habit of leaving bits of food everywhere, and I went searching for her stashes. On top of a cabinet, the previous class had left some artwork made out of beans and other legumes. I noticed a lot of them had been pulled off and some rodent droppings had been left.

I had live traps at home and brought one in—to no avail. We left a trap over a weekend and it was sprung, but no occupant was inside. The class next door—we were adjoined by a shared kitchen where we knew the animal was living—had mostly non-ambulatory students, the most helpless of our range. After a few more weeks and a few more unsuccessful tries, my neighbor took over and got the school maintenance involved. They got the dirty rat that had been living in the bottom drawer of our oven and relieving himself in the oven section.

We tried to rid the appliance of the smell by cooking it out. Bad idea. I attribute that bad idea and my ineffectiveness at catching the rat or dealing with it to my messed-up state of mind.

Here is the whole picture: I was commuting some 40 miles round trip. My husband was commuting 400 miles round trip and was only home on the weekends. My closest neighbor was a quarter mile away, and I didn't know her name at the time. I was used to and needed to be around people and have access to activities that could help take my mind off things. Granted, the house was located in a mountain-like atmosphere, and many people came to the area to be calmed, but it didn't help me at the time. I felt worse at home with lots of time to beat myself up for all my mistakes.

A Special Calling ...

It was the year after 9/11 and the whole country was still in shock and pain.

My helpers didn't understand my emotional condition, and it was too complex to explain. The students were much bigger than I had had before and more physically capable of hurting someone. Safety was always job one in my room.

Underlying it all—during the good years—I had assistants—both men—to whom I had grown attached. The two of them balanced out my natural depression, which was not being treated at the time. When they moved on, I felt terribly alone and abandoned. That was the deepest feeling in my being—abandonment. All my life I had carried that feeling deep inside. Add menopause, and there you have one messed up inner turmoil.

Then the treatment for the menopause turned out to cause as many problems as it solved.

TOBY—A TRAGEDY

At Toby's funeral Martha, the former manager of his group home, walked up to me, righteous indignation pouring from her small stature, and said,

"I hope you burn in hell."

She had no way of knowing I was in the midst of exactly that. My soul was in a torturous state caused by a lifetime practice of denial, calloused over rage, and a mild case of PTSD. I had a recurring dream of being attacked and when I tried to scream –nothing came out.

I attributed Martha's statement to the odd things people say at funerals; however, it took a long time, maybe 10 years, for me to discover the most likely reason she said that. She really felt I was responsible for Toby's death. The boy had been born into the most miserable of circumstances, with a body that only complicated all other factors. Client confidentiality kept information about his immediate family closely guarded. There was speculation that his parents were in prison, or in mental institutions, which at that time would mean they were extremely dangerous people. There was also speculation that some if not all of his disabilities were caused by abuse from or neglect by his caregivers during his infancy.

When he came to my classroom, he was 15, blind, and had severe pica. A quirky craving he had was to swallow large metal objects, which had already put him in the hospital at least a dozen times for surgeries on his digestive tract. When in the hospital, he couldn't have sheets or blankets on him because he would ingest them by picking at them continually.

He had a limited vocabulary, liked to laugh, loved to walk, and could find his way through obstacles by using his cane.

I previously mentioned, to test his skill, I used an

obstacle course made of the outdoor lunch tables and sent an assistant to walk with him. Our wall of windows looked out on the quad. I observed him from the room. He slowly and calmly tapped his way to a safe bench and sat down. The assistant was a few steps away and not leading or guiding him in any way.

Toby had temper tantrums scream at us. His tantrums hurt only himself because he would bite his hand when angry and frustrated. He was slow moving under all conditions, even when angry.

His stomach had been mangled enough that the only food he could have was Ensure or Boost. Even so, he didn't have a gastronomy tube when he came to my class. Mainly because he would never have left it alone.

Toby was, for the most part, gentle, quiet, and a favorite of our Regular Ed student friends. We found ways of getting him to giggle several times a day—it always lightened the mood. Even though he was verrrrry sloooowww, he would request to walk when he was bored. It was good for him but not always practical. The other high school students would speak to him and touch him so he could feel their presence when he went out, although it was safer to have him walk when there wasn't an explosion of people on the sidewalks.

We had one girl buddy who came every afternoon and tended to him singularly. She would tickle him and talk to him and listen to his ABCs. He received one-on-one attention.

Upon writing this, the part I played in Toby's death has become clear to me, and Martha's statement was properly aimed. This is what I believe happened:

One day before I left that classroom, I heard Toby gulp hard. But I hadn't seen him pick up anything, and there was nothing near his seat. As we later discovered, he had ingested a five-inch bolt. I had no idea he could actually swallow anything that large and don't know when he grabbed it. The only way that became known was when it was removed from his stomach. That surgery was the cause of his feeding tube being implanted. He was in the hospital several weeks, and I transferred in the meantime, oblivious to the outcome of a moment's inattention. The only fortunate aspect of the situation was that a 'button' had been invented to close the gastronomy and he didn't bother it.

How did he die? The teacher who took my place, over-fed him and his stomach burst. I ignored Martha's comments at the funeral because I wasn't his teacher at the time and I didn't think she knew that. However, had he not swallowed the bolt, the disastrous surgery that led to tube feeding wouldn't have been necessary.

Martha transferred from the group home where several of our students lived. And I had transferred to a classroom with younger children in a different town since I had seen her last. These changes took place in a fairly tight timeframe. I was aware of her change—I don't know if she was aware of mine.

I was acting out in my classroom-- with the 'little kids' and my life, and so burned out already that not much teaching got done. I had found a way to "keep the peace," and that was all I aimed for. Hence, I went back to my high school classroom the following fall. (A chapter dedicated to the pre-school class can be found within this publication.)

George, Toby's teacher at the time, was even more mentally and emotionally unqualified to be in the classroom than I was or had ever been at any time. His contract was bought out at the end of that school year. There were many red flags put up about him, all before I was fully informed about his true nature and before he came to my class. In his defense of some of his actions that crossed the line, I said, "He is new to the entire field" and "We all know how x assistant tries to control the classroom and makes it hard for the teacher." These statements were in response to his throwing video cassettes—not DVDs, video cases, the equivalent of a large shoe with corners—at assistant x. (I remind you I was not in the best frame of mind either at the time.)

At winter break that year, he transferred from the middle school classroom to the high school class I left. We each claimed to need a change. I went to a pre-school; he came to my high school. My former assistants kept me apprised of his behavior, and as time went on I could see that my knee-jerk defense of him had been very wrong.

I made an unannounced visit once and found him being very mean to Mark. Completely ignoring the assistants, who were really trying to help him and keep the students safe.

The day he over-fed Toby was during summer school. My former assistant kept telling him what he was doing was wrong, but he didn't stop. She finally called 911, but Toby died shortly after getting to the hospital.

Toby loved music, loved to throw a ball, say the alphabet, take walks, and swallow large, foreign objects. He was developmentally two or three years old—and we buried him on his 17th birthday.

AN UNFORGETTABLE PERSON

One gray day—it could have been fall or winter or early spring—a ray of sunshine came to our room, and the young man who brought it performed a bit of magic.

Ricky was a volunteer from the psych class in Regular Ed. He had been to our room several times and always showed complete acceptance of all our students. He had started a group on campus called PLUR—which stood for Peace, Love, Unity and Respect. Ricky embodied those qualities in all that he did.

This gloomy day he came with a few other students and brought a wireless mic with built-in amplifier. He said he wanted to share some music with our students, so we gathered them all around the big table. Here is where the magic begins. All my squirmy, loud, perpetual-motion kids stopped rocking, twitching, flapping, or wiggling and became quiet.

My helpers and I held our breaths. I was so absorbed in the magic that I can't remember what songs were sung. One of my students was very intelligent—for my class—and spoke some Spanish but usually chose not to speak at all. Ricky passed the mic to him and he sang beautifully. Each of my students had a turn with the mic, and they all behaved as though they were at a concert at Carnegie Hall. While the mic was passed around, they forgot themselves and shared in each other's experiences, and I had tears rolling down my cheeks.

Ricky was a junior that year, and on the first day of school the following year, I heard something on the radio about five high school kids being killed in an accident the night before. I didn't hear any names or details.

When I got to my school, every high school student I saw was in tears. I had no idea the kids who had died were from my school, and when my assistant told me Ricky was one of them, my heart broke.

Even more of a shock, the accident had happened close to where I lived.

I went to Ricky's memorial, which his family made a true celebration with dance music and embellishments of the time, lots of glow sticks, and strobes.

The day of magic he brought to us, I have stored in a timeless place to be cherished for the rest of my life.

THE STORIES OF THE TWO JO-JOS: ONE HAPPY, ONE TRAGIC

Jolene:

When I'd been there for three school years, we had a 'graduation' party for Jolene, our only student to 'age out' that year.

She was a tiny girl who was ambulatory, non-verbal, and non-aggressive—unless there was pudding around. She could move very quickly when motivated by the sight of pudding.

Her mother reluctantly conceded when I asked if I could buy Jolene—JoJo—a graduation dress.

"I saw this perfect dress, just her size, and it's so beautiful. It comes with a matching hat and purse. Let me send it home with her, and if you don't want her to wear it for graduation, send her in another dress. But please keep the one I'm sending, as I have no other students it will fit."

Her mother replied with hesitancy in her voice, "Well, all right then."

I worked for hours after school, decorating the room. The focal point of the room was the back wall. I formed a heart from two long garlands of pink silk flowers. In the center of the heart was a framed picture of Jolene wearing a graduation robe and mortarboard in the school colors.

The back of the room was the first thing you saw when you walked into our room. The twelve-foot counter space, plus two six-foot folding tables, were loaded with pizzas, salads, sandwiches, cake, and punch. A side table held a guest book.

Family members of Jolene's fellow classmates had brought food and stayed to attend her graduation. When JoJo arrived. she was wearing the dress and hat I had found and, with the addition of a number of her family members, the room felt like an extended family's Thanksgiving.

A young man in his late teens, a cousin, I think, held his head high and beamed when he saw her picture on the back wall. He kept trying to hide his smile and his pride, but he didn't succeed.

After the principal of the school gave our graduate the Certificate of Completion, Jolene's mother changed her daughter's clothes. Wearing a pair of white pedal pushers and a pink blouse, JoJo then opened gifts. One of the gifts was a plastic bat and whiffle ball. She got so excited over it that we took it out of the package, and she toddled to the front of the room and swung the bat a few warm up swings.

We were all dumbstruck. She had never shown such an intense interest in our sports before. But here she was, focused, in a proper stance—also surprising—and when she swung at the ball it was a perfect hit, a slow, high arc. It sailed all the way to the back of the room and landed right in the punchbowl. Bull's eye!

The decibel level of the cheers from those 30 people equaled any you would have found at any other sporting event.

She giggled and took a stance again, ready to swat the ball out of the park. She did.

When it came time to wind things down and cut the cake, I told a Jolene story about the time she moved almost at the speed of light to get to the fridge and snarf the chocolate pudding. I had been temporarily alone—minutes—and one of the boys indicated he needed toileting immediately. I was fast at that task, so I took him into the toilet and changed him in less than 60 seconds.

When I came out, there was no JoJo on her favorite spot! I turned in the other direction and saw the fridge door open. JoJo's shoes could be seen behind the door, but no other part of her. I rushed over to find she had scooped most of the chocolate pudding out of the bowl with her fingers, and she and the floor where she was standing were covered in it.

She had a special walker which she had not used to get over there. I made a note to myself—motivation is everything!

All the mess on the floor and on her was cleaned up before my helpers got back, and they teasingly didn't believe all that I said had happened while they were gone.

Stanley Jo:

Other teachers had scary stories about Stanley Jo. (Jo-Jo) He was big even for a high-schooler. He was tall and muscular, and just looking at him made a person think, "This guy could be dangerous." He had a history of violent outbursts, but when I first met him standing next to his mother, he was medicated and calm. As a matter of fact, he never had a temper tantrum in my classroom. However, he often had them at home, and he and his mother had to move when he broke doors and walls in their apartments. They were one of the poorest of my families.

One day I was about to make some blueberry muffins and was amazed at how alive he became. He stood beside me as I opened the box. "Would you like to help me?" I asked. We worked together: he poured milk, I broke the eggs; he stirred and placed the batter in the paper holders. I added fresh blueberries and he gobbled a handful. I discovered he would do anything for a blueberry muffin, and I gave him the opportunity three times a week.

He was adept with his hands and followed my instructions without rebelling. There were more incidents at home which caused them to move to another county. Before leaving, his mother asked my advice. "I can't control him at all anymore," she admitted. She was truly worried. "He is just too big. I'm afraid he will hurt someone else when he breaks windows and throws furniture out of the house. I don't know what to do."

Here was a critical moment of judgment. I spoke from my head without consulting my heart. Had I consulted my heart, my answer may have been very different.

"You are allowed to call the police when he is a danger to himself or others," I replied in my professionally distant voice.

A few years went by. I transferred to a different area within the district. The local news got my attention when they spoke about an autistic man who had died after being put in a chokehold by the police. It happened in the town they had moved to. The news announcer said Stanley Jo's name, and I went cold all over.

Stanley Jo's mother, her question, and my answer replayed in my mind.

After work, I looked around on the net I found out the story. The mother had called to cancel the police because before they could get there he had calmed down. They came anyway her call was too late. She told the police not to send any more than one person in at a time to his room—they had a 'policy' to send more. Three men his size went into his room they barely all fit. He panicked. They performed a chokehold and he died. I tried to follow the trial but lost track in the dither that being a teacher creates. I don't know if she sued the city—or perhaps the county schools—based upon my advice. I will carry that burden a while longer at least—and maybe to my grave. It is most probable that the city paid her a good sum of money.

Maybe all they needed to do was offer him a blueberry muffin.

MAINSTREAMING AT THE HIGH SCHOOL

At the time, the closest my students could come to being mainstreamed was for some to attend an assembly, go to the library, or visit a classroom for a few minutes, to fulfill an IEP goal.

One of my students—Johnny, as I mentioned before, —dusted shelves in the library. I tried out a few other students for the job, but they didn't work out. There was also a boy who was non-verbal but very savvy, and he was capable of taking a large barrel and a grabber stick and picking up litter all over campus.

We almost had one of our girls join the pep team for a football game. For Halloween, Bianca wore a cheerleader outfit in the school colors. The pep team invited her to come to the game. I sent a note home telling the mother, but Bianca got sick the night of the game.

She was what I call a sleeper. There were a lot of tasks like assembly she couldn't do well. She matched sox and folded laundry pretty well but was limited in capacity for anything higher.

Except—we had a computer program memory game that required remembering where the symbols or items were. All the cards are face down, about 20 of them. The player would click on a card and the game would show a symbol. Click on another card and see another symbol—probably a different symbol than the previous one. The player keeps hunting for matches as the game turns over the cards. After a few weeks of practice, Bianca was as good at it as I was. A hidden talent.

She was a sweet, charming girl who made sounds, gestures, head movements, and inflections as though she were using real words and conversing. She was not, but the effort would cause some people she "talked" with to reply.

She was always dressed fashionably, without being over the top. Her brother applied her make-up and she was cute as a bug, through and through, with a slender figure to die for!

Some students had mainstreaming goals in their IEP's, but keeping with their abilities and interests, they were service-oriented and not in the presence of the overall population.

HEIMLICHS

My students did not make the universal signal that they were choking. Most people grab their throats with both hands, and that alone is an attention-getter that everyone with them understands.

I learned the hard way that Hispanic families may be uninformed regarding the need or process of performing the Heimlich.

Before I came back into the classroom, we had a neighbor with an autistic child. He was about eight. We were living in the fifth-wheel in a mobile home park, so our homes were squeezed together. I often heard the boy running from one end of their trailer to the other for long periods of time. I believe he vocalized, but don't specifically remember. The family was Hispanic and only the father spoke English.

One night while the grandmother was watching the boy, he began running up and down the trailer like he always did. A while later the paramedics came to the house: the boy had choked to death on a piece of sandwich.

The grandmother was devastated. So was I, for being so close—right next door and of no help. When the ambulance came, I was home. I felt I should have done something to prevent the tragedy.

All family members and those who sit with non-verbal people with any malacy that weakens muscles should know how and when to perform the Heimlich. Especially for those who can't indicate the need for it.

***

The school supplied some of the lunches for our students. Hamburgers and burritos were frequently on the menu. It seemed to me to be common sense that, for our students, all the thickly folded, dry portions of the tortilla should be cut off and the rest of the burrito should be cut into small pieces. My assistant forgot to toss the tough part one day. She was talking and laughing while standing next to Bianca, and I watched from across the table, standing next to Zeke, for whom I had done the Heimlich three times in the year.

Bianca spread her arms and grabbed the table with both hands, then began making motions with her mouth like a fish out of water. That was also Zeke's signal for choking. I watched long enough to know that the assistant was unaware, and I hustled around the table and cleared Bianca's throat by the procedure.

***

There is one more story on this subject. In my last years of teaching, there was a boy who was quadriplegic from being oxygen-starved after a child fed him a string bean when my student was only six months old. He choked on it and was undiscovered until it was much too late. He was permanently, severely disabled.

Any teacher, school nurse, caregiver, or caseworker involved with non-verbal people, please be sure everyone who works with the disabled knows how to do the Heimlich. It seems to be even more important if the family is non-English speaking because the information has not gotten to them. If done before the person loses consciousness, it's possible no further damage to their mental faculties may occur.

PREDICTABILITY

Even the most unpredictable students have "tells" that they are unhappy, afraid, confused, or about to blow. Any number of clues can be picked up when you know your student well enough. Some of the precedent actions are a change in pitch, tone, or frequency of sounds, change in the rhythm of pacing or tapping, or self-abusive biting or head slapping. It won't take long to discover these, but you must be observant.

Other predictable behaviors may be surprising. There is the case of a high school girl who had frequent seizures and afterward would laugh and charge around the room, tipping over couches and chairs as she ran haphazardly. We learned to keep her down after a seizure to ensure the safety of the other students and herself. Seizures present themselves in varied and sometimes odd fashions. There was an adult woman who appeared to have two personalities because of the odd way she changed during a seizure.

Most of the time the person will want to sleep if it is a grand mal; the petit mals are not often detected unless a family member is aware enough to recognize them and tell you about it.

The smaller ones, however, usually involve blank stares for extended periods of time and no response when the person's name is called. Such small seizures can happen several times a day without anyone noticing.

Personally, I have never seen anyone bite their tongue during a seizure or be so relaxed that their tongue falls to the back of their throat. Just in case, however, if you see someone, anyone, having a seizure while lying on their back, put them on their side, and if possible put something soft under their head. This prevents the tongue issue and will keep their head from bouncing on hard surfaces with force.

Sadly, I know of two people who have died due to seizures because the person was not medicated properly. Both cases happened when I was working with adults at LOVARC. They died either through their own doing or ignorance on the part of the caretaker. I mentioned one previously, Carlos an inexcusable loss.

The other was a man well known to the police in the community. He had a seizure on the main street in town, face down. Subsequently, he was arrested for being drunk in public. He was drunk in addition to seizing, but the police put him in a concrete cell and, when he had another seizure during the night, he fell on his back and hit his head many times during the seizure.

LITTLE KIDS—A TEMPORARY TRANSFER

I took a break from high school, starting in February of one year and going through summer school I worked with Preschool/Kindergarten level. I got off to a rocky start. I had been to the class only a few days and had five students. However, I live at a high altitude and it snowed that year like it has not snowed since. Being snowed in, I couldn't get to work for two days. When I returned, I had eight students.

The room was shared with another teacher and her aides. My personal life was in shambles, and it showed in my work. Even so, I did the best I could. One boy required a lot of attention. He would suddenly run around the room, tipping over bookcases and other dangerous objects. His previous teacher had had everything screwed to the floor. I only learned of that after he had been in my class for a time. The parents did not want to medicate him and didn't even believe he needed it until his mother actually saw him slap a teacher and run around, shoving other students and generally creating chaos. That was after I left the class.

Several times in my teaching years, I had students who needed meds and the parents didn't believe in them—until the child grew as big or bigger than the parent. An elementary-age student would age out, and when I later saw the family in a store, the student would be perfectly civilized and calm. If I said I was surprised, the parent would confess the child was now medicated. Yet for the years I had had the child, I had been expected to deal with their outbreaks and tantrums. Sigh.

I am not an advocate of drugging every student who

acts up now and then. But those children whom the parents refuse to medicate should have a one-on-one aide—even if it means the parent must be the one.

***

While working with the little kids, one little girl came to my class with seizure meds, and I watched her closely. She appeared to have a seizure and then laid her head on the table to rest. I spoke to her as I walked over to see about her and found she was smiling—not resting. I told her parents I didn't think she needed those meds anymore, and her doctor agreed.

Afterwards, she became more active and brighter in class. She was a joy to work with. The class was mixed half and half between some who would learn and cooperate and those who were a constant source of stress.

***

During the few months I was there, Toby, the boy in the high school class, I talked about previously, died when he was over-fed and his stomach burst.

I failed miserably in the Pre-K class and returned to the high school during the fall. There had been many changes to the makeup of my class, and more were in the works when I returned.

When school started, I discovered Johnny had transferred; I had been looking forward to taking him to the next step and including him more fully with the mainstream population.

There had also been a very capable young man who could do a lot of things on campus. I had intended to get him more involved in the mainstream. He also transferred, and one of my longtime students was beginning to act out daily.

A high school setting had been my assignment for five years. I was definitely getting worn out. My personal life was still a mess, and I had all the symptoms of PTSD.

My room assignment was moved to another city, but I had most of the same students. I couldn't keep assistants, because I didn't utilize them and stressed myself out even further. The student who was acting out came with me. He was nearing 18 and was showing signs that he didn't want to come to school any more. I used his reluctance and pushed him to acting out more with my attitude.

There was also an increase in the number of students—two of them also had tube feedings.

SALLY

When the state was mandated to empty out their large institutions that housed mentally ill and developmentally disabled persons, the younger ones went to group homes, and those still eligible went to school. Sally came to me as my first student with a G-Tube. She was ambulatory but, due to a hip issue, swung her body from side to side rather than standing straight up and moving ahead in a straight line.

She wore a boxing helmet and had a disfiguring scar on her jaw. The helmet and the scar were there because of a habit she had of repeatedly slugging herself on the jaw. However, she would not pull the G-tube out unless it was broken. In that case she would bring it to us to show us it needed to be replaced. There is a window of a couple hours where it must be replaced or the opening that accommodates it will begin to close and surgery may be required to replace it. She was very good when it came to dealing with her tube.

Our first day did not go well. She came to school with a liter-sized plastic bottle she used as a pacifier to keep from hitting herself, which she would do even with the helmet on. I was working with another student when Sally came up behind me and, with a full circular swing, clobbered me on the head with the bottle.

If we took it away, she would stim by hitting herself. If we let her roam around the room with it, we had no way of knowing who she might hit with it. We had had a party a few days before, and there were balloons taped to the walls, high up to keep the students from breaking them and choking on them.

After Sally clobbered me, I let her wander about the room so I could observe her while I stuck to her like glue. The other students seemed to be off limits by her own choosing, and she ignored them. When the balloons caught her eye, she moved very quickly toward them and pointed while making a sound.

I reached up, took one, and handed it to her. Nope, not that one—she refused it with body language. Dissatisfied with my choice, she did something no other student I had would or could ever do... well maybe Wayne. She problem solved with no preliminary demonstration. Grabbing a chair, she stood on it to get to the counter to be able to reach the balloon she wanted. It was purple.

Later an assistant took her outside, and I watched her through the wall of windows. At that time the paved access road behind our room still had cars parked there. Sally moved purposely among them, peering in every window as though casing them. When she saw one that contained a plastic water bottle, she actually tried to get into it.

There were other forms of plastic that she would be pacified with, but the bottles were her number one choice. Some students had specific items that worked like that. Several seemed to be attached to plastic in any form, but a few preferred wire clothes hangers.

Upon Sally's arrival at the group home after coming out of the institution, she was placed on an extensive menu of medications. When she had been there for a few years, they hired a new psychiatrist and he took her off most of the meds.

When we moved to the new high school, we had adjoining rooms with another class. Sally loved to be outside, loved to wander about the room, and enjoyed exploring other rooms. Most of the students in the class next door were non-ambulatory. I was training a new assistant and letting him be her one-on-one for a day to get to know her ways.

He let her go toward the other room, and she sat down in the middle of the doorway between our two rooms.

I told him, "She will stay there forever, and if you try to move her, she can force her body even closer to the floor and you won't be able to move her." He looked at me, disbelieving my prediction. He tried to pull her up. She wouldn't budge. He was a big man, she was slender and didn't weigh much, but she could not be moved if she didn't want to go.

Eventually, I learned what would get her to comply with just about anything. The balloons in grocery stores that are shiny and don't lose air are also attached to plastic stems. Both of those things were major motivators for her, and she would respond when they were taken from her.

During my last year in that class, Sally was being weaned off the G-tube, and we were allowed to give her teaspoons of pudding. When I left, she also no longer needed the helmet and had stopped hitting herself. The modification of her meds seemed to be the solution.

***

My last two years in that class were some of the worst years in my teaching career. I was burned out and not of much use. The students were getting bigger and more aggressive, and I had more of them.

Some of them attacked on a daily basis hitting, biting and kicking. I was still paralyzed when it came to delegating, and my helpers needed to be told what to do. That was not my preferred way of operating.

My expectations were based on the fact that I'd had sub assistants come in— take a look around the room-- and do exactly what needed doing without me having to tell them. Yet, my regulars seemed to need constant direction--which was unworkable with the type of students we had. I really needed people who knew when and where to jump in, or who could see I needed to step out when I didn't have that insight. When I did have one that would step in—they got moved up.

PERMANENT TRANSFER—2004

It was obvious I was in need of a transfer, and the economy in general was requiring teachers on the high end of the scale to take early retirements—something I could not do. However, transferring and getting back to my Faith helped to keep my burnout from getting worse.

The class in transferred into was an elementary class, a relief from the bigger, more aggressive students. There were plenty of behaviors that got on my nerves but no one I had to fight with every day. In fact, I had a few who were the delight I had always imagined having. There were two sisters. One was ten during her first year with me, and one was five. They both had CP, and the five-year-old was very bright. Each had been a twin at birth, and their siblings had died. Two sets of twins to one family and complications at birth left only one twin in each case.

The parents were undocumented, and it was nearly impossible to get my students the assistive equipment they needed. Their wheelchairs were not fitted to them, Medi-Cal was limited in what could be done for them, and they were not eligible for food stamps.

The younger, brighter child wanted and was willing to learn. Her sister was ill a lot, and all her food had to be pureed. Several of the students in the class had to have pureed food. Lunchtimes could be a whole chapter if I wanted to go into it—which I don't and won't.

In all my classes throughout all the years, self-feeding goals were primary in the IEPs. Goals included independently holding spoons, cups, and filling spoons; tolerating different textures of food, and in a rare case or two, making their own sandwiches and pouring their own drinks.

The bright little girl with CP loved to use a switch to operate the blender when we were making a cake or muffins. We adapted other utensils and materials to enable the other students to help in a project.

Sometimes hand-over-hand wiping the table or counters was included.

The site of my new classroom was a building with only two classrooms. They were not attached to or associated in any way with a Regular Ed school; it was just two Special Ed classrooms. During the three years I was there, another classroom was added. Here's why:

TABLE 14-1: Prevalence of ASD in the United States, Based on ADDM Network Studies Published from 2007 to 2014
(surveillance years 2000–2010)

Surveillance Year	Birth Year	Total Population Aged 8 Years Under Surveillance	ASD Prevalence per 1,000 (95% confidence interval)	Approx. 1 in X children
2000	1992	187,761	6.7 (6.3, 7.1)	1 in 150
2002	1994	407,578	6.6 (6.4, 6.9)	1 in 150
2004	1996	172,335	8.0 (7.6, 8.4)	1 in 125
2006	1998	307,790	9.0 (8.6, 9.3)	1 in 110
2008	2000	337,093	11.3 (11.0, 11.7)	1 in 88
2010	2002	363,749	14.7 (14.3, 15.1)	1 in 68

SOURCE: Adapted from http://www.cdc.gov/ncbdd/autism/data.html. (accessed July 15, 2015).

From: 14 - Prevalence of Autism Spectrum Disorder Mental Disorders and Disabilities Among Low-Income Children.

Committee to Evaluate the Supplemental Security Income Disability Program for Children with Mental Disorders; Board on the Health of Select Populations; Board on Children, Youth, and Families; Institute of Medicine; Division of Behavioral and Social Sciences and Education; The National Academies of Sciences, Engineering, and Medicine; Boat TF, Wu JT, editors.

Washington (DC): National Academies Press (US); 2015 Oct 28.

Copyright 2015 by the National Academy of Sciences. All rights reserved.

NCBI Bookshelf. A service of the National Library of Medicine, National Institutes of Health.

Key Findings: Trends in the Prevalence of Developmental Disabilities in U. S. Children, 1997–2008

Researchers from the Centers for Disease Control and Prevention (CDC), in collaboration with researchers from the Health Resources and Services Administration (HRSA), have published a new study in Pediatrics: "Trends in the Prevalence of Developmental Disabilities in U.S. Children, 1997–2008." This study determined the prevalence of developmental disabilities in U.S. children and in selected populations for a 12-year period. The findings from this article are summarized in the following text.

Main Findings from This Study:

Data from the study showed that developmental disabilities (DDs) are common: about 1 in 6 children in the U.S. had a DD in 2006–2008. These data also showed that prevalence of parent-reported DDs has increased 17.1% from 1997 to 2008. This study underscores the increasing need for health, education and social services, and more specialized health services for people with DDs.

"Learn the Signs. Act Early." Program:

Identifying developmental disabilities early allows children and their families to get the help they need. You can follow your child's development by watching how he or she plays, learns, speaks, and acts. Talk with your child's doctor at every visit about the milestones your child has reached and what to expect next. Learn more at www.cdc.gov/actearly.

- The prevalence of any DD in 1997–2008 was 13.87%
  - Prevalence of learning disabilities was 7.66%;
  - Prevalence of attention deficit hyperactivity disorder (ADHD) was 6.69%;
  - Prevalence of other developmental delay was 3.65%; and,
  - Prevalence of autism was 0.47%.
- Over the last 12 years, the
  - Prevalence of DDs has increased 17.1%—that's about 1.8 million more children with DDs in 2006–2008 compared to a decade earlier;
  - Prevalence of autism increased 289.5%;
  - Prevalence of ADHD increased 33.0%; and,
  - Prevalence of hearing loss decreased 30.9%.
- In addition, data from this study showed
  - Males had twice the prevalence of any DD than females and more specifically had higher prevalence of ADHD, autism, learning disabilities, stuttering/stammering and other DDs;
  - Hispanic children had lower prevalence of several disorders compared to non-Hispanic white and non-Hispanic black children, including ADHD and learning disabilities;
  - Non-Hispanic black children had higher prevalence of stuttering/stammering than non-Hispanic white children;
  - Children insured by Medicaid had a nearly two-fold higher prevalence of any DD compared to those with private insurance; and,
  - Children from families with income below the federal poverty level had a higher prevalence of DDs.

To better understand why the prevalence has increased, future research should focus on understanding the influence of increases in the prevalence of known risk factors, changes in acceptance and awareness of conditions, and benefits of early intervention services.

About Developmental Disabilities and this Study:

Developmental disabilities are a diverse group of severe chronic conditions that are due to mental and/or physical impairments. People with developmental disabilities have problems with major life activities such as language, mobility, learning, self-help, and independent living. Developmental disabilities begin anytime during development up to 22 years of age and usually last throughout a person's lifetime.

For this study, researchers aimed to determine the prevalence of DD in U.S. children overall and in certain populations from 1997–2008. Researchers analyzed responses from the 1997–2008 National Health Interview Surveys. A total of 119,367 children ages 3–17 were included in the study. Parents or legal guardians were asked if their child had any of the following conditions: ADHD, autism, blindness, cerebral palsy, moderate to profound hearing loss, intellectual disability, learning disorders, seizures, stuttering/stammering, and other developmental delay.

Developmental Disabilities—CDC Activities:

CDC is part of a larger group of public and private organizations working to better understand developmental disabilities through surveillance, research, and early identification. CDC is undertaking efforts to:

- study how common developmental disabilities are and who is more likely to have them;
- find the causes of developmental disabilities and the factors that increase the chance that a person will have one; and,

- learn how people with developmental disabilities can improve the quality of their lives.

***

The transfer helped relieve some stress and it didn't get any worse. But I carried the burn-out with me. It was a true blessing to have children that were smaller, less aggressive, and even fun to work with. My students still had behavior issues, some of which were unnerving and frustrating to deal with. The noises were the hardest part, but one little girl was intent on masturbating every time we put her on the toilet. She was blind and had very little outside stimuli. We were working on teaching her to use a blind person's cane—but without much luck.

To ease the stress and overcome the noise, we spent a lot of time outside and doing art when we were inside.

I EXPECTED SOMETHING MAGICAL

My last day after my return to teaching was as insignificant as the first day—remember? I expected something "magical" to happen when I unlocked the door. Nothing magical happened when I locked my last classroom door for the last time.

All the magic had occurred the year before in the spring. The teacher next door was surprised to discover she was pregnant—with twins. She had already adopted an autistic boy who had been her student and had all but given up on having children of her own.

But that spring there were many confirmations that life was going on in a big way.

We had a pair of ground-nesting birds nest on our school grounds. There was another nest over the back door of my classroom, as well as several caterpillars, which led to the delivery van driving through thousands of butterflies a few months later on his way to the farthest site for his job.

The renewal of that spring was inspiring and refreshing, to be sure. It still took years for the PTSD to leave me. During the time it was still with me, I couldn't write these stories. The door to the pain and stress and guilt and grief opened wide and I just couldn't do it.

Now that I have, I have to wonder, *"Where are the good, quiet, joyful days? Days of music, dancing, kite flying from Phillip's chair; the piñatas we made and broke just for fun at the high school? What about the days of progress so dramatic we all jumped up and down in celebration? Were they too few to mention or were they over-shadowed by maintaining a safe environment or keeping angry parents at bay while holding onto my somewhat fragile sanity?*

A Special Calling ...

    My husband retired in 2004 after commuting to the central coast, while I was living in 'our' house some 200 miles away. I was still teaching for 3 more years to build up my retirement allotment. We enjoy each other's company and travel while we still can.

    And I write—about whatever helps me heal and makes my heart happy, happy, happy.

www.ingramcontent.com/pod-product-compliance
Lightning Source LLC
Chambersburg PA
CBHW032136040426
42449CB00005B/269